HOW TO LIVE & '

1 1.00

/13

In this Series

LIVE & WORK IN SPAIN

A Handbook for Short and Long Stay Visitors

Robert A C Richards

How To Books

To Myrtle Allen of Fowey, Cornwall, with thanks again for giving
me the first lesson in writing.

Note: The author has sought to ensure accuracy and sound advice at the time of
writing, but legislation changes as do 'times and tides' in Spain as elsewhere. So
readers are urged to check for regional and local adaptations to the national norm. No
responsibility can be accepted for any actions resulting from reading this book.

© Copyright 1992 by Robert A C Richards

First published in the UK in 1992 by How To Books Ltd, Plymbridge House,
Estover Road, Plymouth PL6 7PZ, United Kingdom.
Tel: Plymouth (0752) 705251. Fax: (0752) 695699. Telex: 45635.

A catalogue record for this book is available from the British Library.

Typeset by Kestrel Data, Exeter
Printed and bound by The Cromwell Press Limited, Melksham, Wiltshire

Contents

List of Illustrations

Preface

Is Spain different?

Read on in a book as different as Spain itself because it is based on the experiences of a full-time journalist who has lived in Spain since 1963.

This book will detail the realities of 'living and working in Spain', and describe the many differences which make life more pleasant.

Customs in Spain are different, for example the Spanish preference for eating a light breakfast and large late lunch and dinner. Amando de Miguel explains in his book *Los Españoles*, that it stems from the desire to be different from the peasants who ate a hearty breakfast and went to bed early. Many of these customs are fully described to help you become attuned to a new life-style which is very much to the liking of many. Needless to say, it is much easier to appreciate life in Spain as a retired person enjoying the many amenities but many helpful tips are included for those who intend to work, as well.

Regional variation is another of Spain's big differences. While avalanches are sweeping down in the Pyrenees you may be enjoying the sea and sun on the Costa del Sol or in the Canary Islands. These differences are also described.

Before you come, however, remember to obtain a Spanish visa from your local Spanish consulate and pay some money into a Spanish bank so that you can apply for a residential permit and/or a work permit.

This book pulls no punches, but shows the real *España*. Reading this may spare you many expenses and unpleasant experiences and will help you fit comfortably into the Spanish way of life.

Robert A. C. Richards

Fig. 1. Spain: provinces and main cities

1
Welcome to Spain

You will be made to feel welcome when you arrive in Spain. The customs officer at the border will smile at your children—they are the rulers of the roost throughout Spain. The taxi driver at the airport is often a mine of information and the climate smiles, too. Gone are the days of 'rain spreading from the west' as day upon day of cloudless skies dawn.

The Spanish way of life offers everything from classical guitar played in ancient castles to a multitude of modern hyper and supermarkets. In Madrid and many other cities, ancient monuments cluster next to modern high-rise buildings, although nowadays care is taken to protect these memories of a vast, ancient and well documented history. Streams of different peoples have left their permanent mark from the Iberos of uncertain origin to the Romans who provided monuments in every part of the Peninsula. The Spanish saga includes the Visigoths, a surprisingly long Arab occupation, and the *restoración* when the northern kingdoms finally completed the domination of Spain in 1492.

IS SPAIN FOR YOU?

When planning any project, it is good to sit down in a quiet corner to determine exactly what is involved. Here are a few really basic questions worth considering.

Living in Spain
● Do I want a better climate—and can I stick the weather?

● Can I adapt to the Spanish timetable with its late lunch and evening meal and shopping hours which last until 22.00?

● Am I fond of company or do I have a Greta Garbo complex?—both can be accommodated.

- Can I adapt to the extrovert life, so very different from the Northern European reserve?

- Can I learn a foreign language when I have so many other commitments? (You will never be able to enjoy living and working in Spain to the full unless you do!)

Working in Spain
- Would I be prepared to work in the evening?

- Could I adapt to a variable working timetable?

- Would I be prepared to work non-stop from 08.00 or 09.00 until 15.00 (*horario intensivo*) during the very hot summer months?

- Could I work the standard multinational timetable, when the rest of the country is operating on a different wavelength?

The quirks of the country
Spain is different in many unexpected ways from other countries. The next chapter is devoted to a detailed description of just *how* different. You should consider it carefully when making your decision.

THE ADVANTAGES OF LIVING IN SPAIN

The Roman influence
Long before the Arabs came to conquer Spain in the eighth century, the Romans had discovered many of the fine points of the country. Their villa sites are located in pleasant areas besides rivers and coasts. Remains can be seen in every part of Spain from the leafy greenness of Asturias to Mérida with its impressive theatre, amphitheatre and aqueduct. The entire Iberian Peninsula was under Roman domination for many centuries and it extends into place names to this day.

Some modern Spanish place names remain unchanged like Segovia, others are similar like Tarragona, originally Tarraco, and Málaga, formerly Malaca. Others are completely different but that is not to say that the Roman names have fallen out of use. If someone tells you he is '*complutenses*', it is not contagious; he means that he is a native of Alcalá de Henares. They are also used in written Spanish in lower case as above. This is the correct *castellano* (the very best Spanish which is spoken in the region of that name, particularly in the cities of Valladolid, Palencia and the ancient university of Salamanca). Here is a table to help you identify these places.

Modern city name	Roman city name	Spanish adjective
Alicante	Lucentum	lucentines
Astorga	Asturica Augusta	asturicenses
Cádiz	Gades	gaditanos
Calahorra	Calagurris	calagurritanos
Calatayud	Bilbilis	bilbilitanos
Ecija (Seville)	Astigi	astigitanos
Elche (Alicante)	Ilici	ilicenses
Gerona	Gerunda	gerundenses
Gibraltar	Calpe	calpetanos
Huelva	Onuba	onubenses
Huesca	Osca	oscenses
Jativa	Saetabis	setabitanos
Lérida	Ilerda	ilerdenses
Lugo	Lucus Augusti	lucenses
Málaga	Malaca	malacitanos
Mérida	Emerita Augusta	emeritenses
Palencia	Palantia	palentinos
Salamanca	Salmantica	salmanticenses
Segorbe (Castellón)	Segobriga	segorbinos
Seville	Hispalis	hispalenses
Tarragona	Tarraco	tarraconcenses

Whether you are in Spain for a long or short stay it should be remembered that it has a massive mainland—491,205 square kilometres—with a wildly different character in each of its seventeen provinces. The exploration of inland Spain is simple and well worth the time and effort. The wide variation of regional characteristics is a true part of the 'Spain is different' claim of so many travel posters. Compare this to the statement made by a Greek gentleman—'We have visited every part of the British Isles, and it's all the same. The architecture is the same in Scotland as in Cornwall, with Marks and Spencers everywhere, and a standardised form of housing'. Although much the same could be said of the modern parts of Spanish cities, there is usually an extensive ancient portion as well which is full of individuality.

The *Costas* are so well documented in travel literature of every sort that there seems little point in repeating them. Instead the unique qualities of the fifty provinces in Spanish territory will be noted here.

The provincial capital cities all have the same layout. There will be the ancient centre with its medieval buildings, often including a *Parador Nacional* (State-run hotel), surrounded by a pleasant modern shopping centre. Then, on the outskirts, there will be the uniform blocks of flats and even a few detached houses. Until recently the Spanish have always considered the community life of modern high-rise flats as the most desirable form of residence but these days the latest craze is for separate housing. These range from matchbox units in terraces to luxury detached dwellings.

If you prefer to visit areas less well known to foreigners try the north-west where the historic cities of Avila, Salamanca, Zamora, Orense and Pontevedra are to be highly recommended for their highly individual character.

Here is a quick guide to a few select provinces.

Extremadura
The cities of Cáceres and Badajoz are well worth seeing as are other 'ancient jewels' such as Mérida (founded by the Romans in 25 BC as Augusta Emerita and also known as the 'Rome of Spain'), Zafra, Guadalupe, Trujillo, Alcántara, Plasencia, Ciudad Rodrigo.

Cataluña
As Cataluña is one of the most industrialised parts of Spain, it is not surprising that you have to travel a certain distance to escape from its development but the country areas are very pleasant. The ancient homes of gentleman farmers have frequently been converted into luxury restaurants serving the traditional cuisine in high cool rooms. The *Paradores Nacionales* (State hotels and PN for short) are to luxury standards, thus indicating a good tourist area. PN Vic(h) overlooks lakes, and is located in quiet, wooded countryside . . . postcode 08500. Tel: (93) 888 72 11, fax: (93) 888 73 11. The PN of Cardona is an impressive castle with fine views . . . postcode 08261, Tel: (93) 869 12 75, fax: (93) 869 16 36.

Barcelona
Barcelona caters for every taste. There are ample beaches nearby, an extensive marina in the port, boat trips and motor racing at Montjuich, the huge new Olympic village. Its nightlife is famed

for its catholic appeal, from classical concerts and the best opera singers, jazz festivals and rock and roll concerts to the guitars in the cafes and the litre sized glasses of beer to be bought in the old plaza near the port. The Catalans may be famous for their hardworking characteristics but they also know how to enjoy themselves.

The city of Barcelona offers a great deal to the visitor or resident. The port area attracts many to see the replica of Columbus' ship, enjoy the palm-lined gardens and sample the *tapas* in the bars. You can climb to the top of Columbus' statue, erected on the site near the Placa del Rei where he is reputed to have given his first report after his return home to the *Reyes Católicos* (The Catholic Monarchs). Guidebooks and booklets are as numerous as editions of foreign newspapers here and they will tell you all about it. Museums abound. The Poble Espanyol is another very interesting place. Here you will find each region of Spain represented by a house built in the traditional, regional style of that province. From these houses you can buy goods traditionally associated with the provinces.

Nevertheless, the very high temperatures and humidity enjoyed in the hottest months of July and August can make staying in Barcelona very unpleasant. You can make plenty of trips out though to escape the conditions.

The coastline
The coast is the obvious choice in the hottest months. It is the choice of many Catalans, too, so expect traffic jams at peak periods. Blanes marks the start of the *Costa Brava* (Wild Coast), so-called because there are so many storms in the winter. To the north there are many *calas* (rocky coves) with clear waters and bright sands. Blanes is 106 kms from Barcelona and offers fine beaches and the Marimurtra. This is not a tame dragon but a botanical garden with over three thousand species of flora. It overlooks the rocky coast and is an ideal place to enjoy the sea breeze. Its name means 'sea and myrtle'.

Blanes is the place where the coastal scenery changes. To the south, there is flat country and rather unattractive beaches; to the north lie the many coastal resorts so well served by the charter airport of Gerona. It may be very difficult to find enough space just to sit down in Tossa de Mar but the tourists continue to flock in their thousands. Lloret de Mar is pleasant as is the ancient port

Fig 2. Barcelona street plan

and holiday resort of Pálamos. For sheer five star luxury, the PN of S'Agaro is to be recommended. The coastal road may not have been designed for busy travellers but the constantly changing views are delightful. Rosas is a large resort with a good beach and a fishing village.

Cadaques was the hometown of the surrealist painter Salvador Dali. It is isolated by twisty roads but worth visiting. The old theatre where Dali held his first exhibition as a teenager has been converted into a museum in his honour. It is as eccentric as the painter's own creations. The opening hours are just as eccentric, from 17.00 until 21.00 on alternate days. There is a complicated schedule of guided tours so if you plan to visit this museum you would be well advised to telephone in advance.

South of Barcelona the beaches are long and flat and there are variety of resorts. Castelldefels has pleasant housing developments and little else. Sitges, however is an older resort with its own character, good beaches (topless), and a reputation for being the place to go. Villanueva y Geltrú is a small family resort with a large fishing port where many foreign concerns are investing. Tarragona is a bustling provincial capital with good beaches, many hotels, and an impressive Roman theatre.

For those who enjoy motorway travel, Peñíscola and Sagunto are ancient cities, very pleasant and full of history. Vinaroz is an unpretentious family seaside resort. Its weekly street market is remarkable for the low prices of local, freshly harvested fruit and vegetables.

Andorra

Although this is a principality and not part of Spain it must be mentioned. Some 50,000 people live here in tax-free glory. Some residents claim to get to Barcelona in two and a half hours using the Cadi tunnel. When the new motorway linking Barcelona and Manresa is finished, this may come down even more. Besides being a mecca for tax-free shopping, Andorra has utopian mountain valleys, excellent skiing stations, and many other attractions— especially its tax-free status. There is a PN at Seo de Urgel which boasts an impressive interior patio hung with plants and you can also enjoy a swim in the indoor swimming pool. This hotel incorporates the cloisters of a monastery. The postcode is 25700. Tel: (973) 35 20 00, fax: (973) 35 23 09.

ANDALUCIA

Seville is the other city for which great things are planned in 1992. A World Exhibition is being held here and a multi-million invasion expected. In anticipation, the Hotel Alfonso the Twelfth, first built for another giant exhibition held in 1928, is being totally re-furbished at a cost of 2,000 million pesetas to full five star, super-luxury standards by Ciga Hotels España. The city of Seville can keep you busy sight-seeing for many days but Andalucía with its white villages, *bodegas* (wine cellars) and folk-lore has its attractions too.

Among the numerous Roman remains to be seen are the ruins of Italica, only 7 kms to the north of Seville, and the necropolis at Carmona.

Ecija, 89 kms to the east of Seville is known as *la sartén de Andalucía* (the frying-pan of Andalucía). It lives up to its name with temperatures of 50°C in the shade in July and August. The heat is something to consider if you do plan a trip to the Exhibition and is something most guidebooks neglect. If you like the heat, and want to see eggs literally fried on the pavement, then visit Ecija in high summer when the *astigitanos* will be glad to give you a demonstration. Otherwise the best months are April and October.

In Jerez de la Frontera there are many *bodegas* which welcome visitors, and the Equestrian School which, though perhaps not to the standard of Vienna, gives demonstrations of horsemanship and the stables can be visited afterwards. Arcos de la Frontera is a picturesque town. Cádiz is an ancient port and city whose narrow streets give a welcome to all and can be seen by horsedrawn carriage.

Ronda just must be seen by anyone visiting Andalucía. A spectacular bridge links the two rocky headlands on which the town is built and there is the oldest bull ring in Spain. It is an ancient town with streets of excellent restaurants such as the Don Pedro. The Hotel Victoria is furnished in a severely English style and has a palm-shaded garden commanding a spectacular view of the valley below and the river Guadelevin. On the floor of the gorge between the two parts of the town lie the ruins of *la Casa del Rey Moro* (the house of the Moorish King) from which Christian prisoners were made to carry water to the town up 365 stairs, a height of 100 metres—hence the saying and curse: *'en Ronda mueras acarreando'*, ('May you die in Ronda carrying water barrels').

There are other cities in Andalucía which really should be

visited, the most usual being Granada, Córdoba and Málaga. Doñana is a nature reserve of over 80,000 hectares, where you can see wild boars, lynx, deer, many rare birds, huge flocks of migrating flamingos, sand-dune 'creep', long unspoilt beaches, pine forests and all sorts of other wildlife. What you see largely depends on the time of year so it is better to check in advance if you wish to visit.

The headquarters building is open every day except Monday from 08.00 until 19.00. You can enjoy a guided tour by Land-rover for 2,000 pesetas per person but you must book in advance. The address is El Acebuche, Coto Doñana (Huelva), Tel: (955) 43 04 32.

Columbus and 1992

At the Monasterio de la Rabida near Palos de la Frontera, Christopher Columbus awaited the backing of the *Reyes Católicos* for his westerly voyage to the Americas. Most of the original monastery was destroyed in an earthquake in the seventeenth century but the existing one is pleasant. A priest will take you on a guided tour and tell you all about that famous day, October 12th 1492, when a cannon shot from Columbus' flagship, *La Pinta*, echoed across an empty ocean. It signalled the first landfall and changed the rest of the world for ever.

Thus 1992 is a very important year for Spain.

A voyage to repeat Columbus' original journey is planned. Replicas of the three ships will sail from Puerto de Palos on August 3rd 1992 and will follow, as far as possible, the same route and take the same length of time, weather and tides permitting.

There are also the 1992 Olympics in Barcelona and the World Exhibition in Seville, the first since Osaka in 1970.

DAILY LIFE

The Spanish timetable has much to recommend it. Whenever you wish for refreshment, whatever the time, it is almost always possible to find somewhere, particularly in the cities where there are 24 hour services. Even in the smaller towns, many catering establishments are open from 06.00 until midnight—unless it is the local closing day. Spanish barmen work at a speed second to none; they really try to please and earn every bit of their free time.

Cafe society

This is very much a part of living in Spain. The entire family will go to the nearest bar or cafe, from the youngest to the oldest, to enjoy a drink and the evening breeze. Sometimes the family go for a full Sunday meal after which a siesta is essential. The Spanish love to talk and this greatly extends their mealtimes. However the average Spaniard believes that time should be his servant rather than his master and the Mediterranean attitude of not worrying too much about the future prevails.

Taxation in Spain
Rates of taxation are still lower in Spain than in many countries. Tax on an average middle class income may still be lower than in the UK. Social security however is quite high. The tax and social security contributions on the average income of an employee are shown in illustration 3 on page 21. It works out much better, however, for the self-employed.

If you are self-employed you must declare all the income you have earned from whatever country if you stay in Spain for more than 183 days. You will have to pay twenty percent tax on it but in the next year the *Hacienda* (tax office) will refund half of it. In this way, after many moons, real taxation works out at ten percent, and you have a compulsory saving scheme.

Since the EEC seems determined to standardise taxation this will doubtless change for the worse. Remember too that all income is taxed even pensions.

Taxes on cars and boats are usually lower in Spain than in other countries. There are no hidden taxes on televisions or radios either. Some homes boast a dozen radios and more, with a television set for every member of the family.

Service charges
Bills for water, rates, electricity and so on are often lower than in northern Europe. However if you decide to buy a flat it is better to choose one with separate heating rather than the very expensive collective heating systems used by some communities of proprietors. Community of proprietors (*comunidad de proprietarios*) is the term used for all the owners of apartments or flats in one building and they are subject to much legislation about which there are many books.

Rubbish is collected every day of the week except Sunday and you have to pay a small fee for the service. If you need a photocopy you will find a machine in most newsagents as well as in the special shops which offer reductions in price.

Fig. 3.   A typical Spanish monthly payslip showing salary for the month, with
social security and taxation deductions. *Sueldo base* = base salary. *Complemento
P. Voluntario* = extras. *Complemento E.Horario* = punctuality bonus. *Antigüedad*
= time with company. *Bolsa vacaciones* = holiday fund. *Total devengado* = grand
total.

DELEGACION DE HACIENDA DE
TOWN

ADMINISTRACION DE HACIENDA DE
CITY OR PROVINCE

MINISTERIO DE ECONOMIA Y HACIENDA

Código Administración

IMPUESTO SOBRE LA RENTA DE LAS PERSONAS FISICAS

PAGO FRACCIONADO

(Empresarios, profesionales y artistas)

DOCUMENTO DE INGRESO

130

130100091508 5

EJERCICIO *YEAR*

PERIODO *QUARTER*

PUT: 1T/2T/3T/or 4T

Espacio reservado para la etiqueta identificativa

N.I.F. = *TAX NUMBER*   APELLIDOS Y NOMBRE O RAZON SOCIAL *SURNAME AND NAMES*

CALLE, PLAZA, ETC   NOMBRE DE LA VIA PUBLICA *ADDRESS*   NUMERO   ESC.   PISO   PRTA.   TELEFONO

MUNICIPIO   PROVINCIA   COD. POSTAL

A Empresarios en Estimación Objetiva Singular (SISTEMA SIMPLIFICADO)
Volumen de ventas desde el inicio del ejercicio ....
RENDIMIENTO NETO 1
CUOTA (10% de clave 1) 2

B Empresarios, Profesionales o Artistas en Estimación Objetiva Singular (SISTEMA NORMAL)
Ingresos desde el inicio del ejercicio ....
RENDIMIENTO NETO² *NET EARNINGS* 3   *OR INCOME*
CUOTA (20% de clave 3) *QUOTA TO PAY* 4   *20% OF ABOVE*

C Empresarios, Profesionales o Artistas en Estimación Directa
Ingresos desde el inicio del ejercicio ....
RENDIMIENTO NETO 5
CUOTA (20% de clave 5) 6
TOTAL CUOTAS (2 + 4 + 6) 7
Retenciones efectuadas 8
Pagos fraccionados realizados 9
TOTAL A INGRESAR (Diferencia 7-8-9) 10

(¹) Para el cálculo de la cuota y de los RENDIMIENTOS NETOS ver instrucciones

□ Negativa

Si la Liquidación correspondiente a este tributo, por el ejercicio y periodo consignado, resulta NEGATIVA, marque con una X el recuadro al efecto. En este caso deberá enviar la copia amarilla a su Delegación o Administración de Hacienda, bien por CORREO CERTIFICADO o mediante ENTREGA PERSONAL.

Ingreso efectuado a favor del TESORO PUBLICO, cuenta restringida de la DELEGACION DE HACIENDA para la RECAUDACION de los TRIBUTOS

FORMA DE PAGO:
□ E.C. En efectivo   □ E.C. Adeudo en cuenta

Importe: I *AMOUNT TO PAY*

CODIGO CUENTA CLIENTE (CCC) — Entidad   Ofic.   DC   Núm. de cuenta

Fecha = *DATE*   Firma *SIGNATURE*

Este documento no será válido sin la certificación mecánica o, en su defecto, firma autorizada

Fig. 4. Tax Form 130 for the self-employed. The form costs 25 ptas. *Rendimiento neto* = net earnings. The self-employed person will normally complete just section B, paying a quota of 20% tax.

SOME DISADVANTAGES

General grumbles range from the deficiencies of the telephone service to the worst public services in Europe. Talking to local people is the best way to discover specific drawbacks. The next chapter will give you a good idea of some of the major differences of Spain and some of the trials you will face if you work in Spain.

Fraud
This has been brought to a very fine art in Spain. Robbery is the most likely to trouble you whether it is someone trying to sell you yesterday's newspaper or your shopping trolley moving away all by itself. Thefts of car radios and cars are commonplace as are burglaries. Constant vigilance and precautionary action go a long way towards counteracting this.

Lying is a way of life in Spain, so do not believe everything you are told. Whether the result of the official religion promulgating 'the pious lie' for so many centuries or part of the third world mentality that still exists in much of Spain, the practice is common and expertly carried out. It is extremely trying to come up against it in officialdom.

More information about the country
One way to prepare for your move is to obtain the local English language publications and read them carefully. These will give you the 'pros and cons'. Here are a few addresses:-

● *Costa Blanca Post and Mail*, Avda. Puerto de Santa Maria 3, 03710 Calpe (Alicante). Tels: (96) 583 51 61, 583 51 96, fax: (96) 585 83 61. English weekly.

● *Costa Blanca News*, Apartado 95, 03500 Benidorm (Alicante). Tels: (96) 585 52 82/7, fax: (96) 585 83 61. English weekly.

● *Journal la Gaviota*, Apartado 2013, 03500 Benidorm (Alicante) —office at El Centro, Avda. de Europa. Tel: (96) 680 38 86, fax: (96) 680 21 02. French bi-monthly.

● *Mallorca Magazin*, calle San Felio 17, 07012 Palma de Mallorca. Tels: (971) 71 61 10, 72 42 46, fax: (971) 719706. German.

● *Majorca Daily Bulletin*, calle San Felio 17, 07012 Palma de Mallorca. Tels: (971) 71 61 10, 72 42 46, fax: (971) 719706. English.

● *Guia d'Andorra*, PO Box 135, Principat d'Andorra. Tel: 26770. English, French, *castellano* and Catalan quarterly with free subscription.

- *Editur International*, Gran Via Carlos III 86-7, 08208, Barcelona. Tel: (93) 330 70 52, fax: (93) 330 74 96.
  Also in UK—Ms Maureen Wingham, 2 Highgate Avenue, London N6. Tel: (071) 384 9111, telex: 29873.
  Also in Paris, Bangkok, and Tokyo. English monthly.

- *Marbella Club Magazine*. Hand Made Magazines SA, calle Prats de Molló 16, 08021 Barcelona. Tel: (93) 414 13 44. Seasonal.

- *Spain Gourmetour*, Paseo de la Castellana 14, 28046 Madrid. Tel: (91) 431 12 40, fax: (91) 431 61 28.

- Iberian Daily Sun, calle Zurban. 74, Madrid. Tel: (091) 442 77 00. English.

- *Sur in English*. Avda. Doctor Marañon 48, 29009 Málaga. Tel: (952) 39 39 00, telex: 79013 MLGA E, fax: (952) 27 95 04. English weekly with excellent coverage.

- *La Gazette Magazine*, Apartado 574, 03590 Altea (Alicante). Tel: (96) 579 46 77.

- *Costa Golf*, calle Loma de los Riscos 1, Apartado 358, 29620 Torremolinos (Málaga). Tel: (952) 38 15 42, fax: (952) 38 15 69.

- *Marbella Times Monthly Magazine*, calle Alonso de Ojeda 2, Carretera de Cádiz km 188, Marbella (Málaga). Tels: (952) 82 21 12, 82 18 73, 82 20 29, fax: 82 20 42. English.
  Also in the UK: 43, Oxford Street, London, W1R 1RD. Tel: (071) 439 7282, fax: (071) 434 11 01.

- *Island Gazette Magazine*, calle Iriarte 43, Puerto de la Santa Cruz, Tenerife, Canary Islands. English.

- *Lookout Monthly Magazine*, Puebla Lucia, Fuengirola (Málaga). English.

SOME HIGHLY RECOMMENDED TRIPS

These trips are based on the city of Madrid. You can either stay in Madrid and make a series of excursions on a daily basis or make slightly longer trips staying overnight. Where possible, accommodation has been recommended. If you visit any of these places you will be sure to discover the real *España*. Descriptions of places are given in case you are short of time and may only see a few of them.

Madrid
This city has been the capital of Spain since 1606 and has acquired many palaces, museums, parks and avenues over the years. The Retiro park is ideal for a lunchtime snack in the summer months, and is well policed. The Prado museum houses the finest collection of Spanish paintings in the world, and the Royal Palace is impressive, used solely for occasions of State. The King lives in a modest palace on the outskirts—the Zaruela.

Toledo
Toledo captures the essence of inland Spain with a wealth of ancient buildings, including two synagogues which are well worth visiting. El Greco's house can be visited and many other monuments. The famous Alcázar began as a fortress in Roman times and was nearly destroyed in the Civil War when it withstood a seventy-two day siege.

El Escorial
The huge royal palace is usually described as a monastery and was built by Felipe II between 1563 and 1584. It gives the impression of massive and ageless strength, the main buildings covering a rectangle of 207 by 161 metres. There is a museum beneath it which demonstrates the construction methods of the time: models of wooden cranes used to hoist huge blocks of stone into place and the original tools. The palace has many important works of art and a famous library.

There are several mini-palaces worth seeing too. There is one near the railway station and another on the road to Avila. It is pleasant to wander about this little town with its open-air cafes and restaurants of all grades, and La Herreria, the park. The Hotel Miranda Suiza makes a pleasant place to stay.

El Escorial is about 1,000 metres above sea level and can make a pleasant change in the summer from Madrid which is only some 600 metres above sea level. The surrounding mountains are covered with pines and are good hiking and walking country. So is the Sierra de Malagón.

Close to El Escorial is the Valle de los Caídos. This is the impressive burial site of General Franco. He lies under a huge

Fig. 6.   Madrid Street Plan

granite slab in an interment on the scale of a Pharaoh. Some of his followers treat the tomb as a shrine.

Incidentally, in winter, El Escorial is well known for icy winds which rush down the mountain sides causing snowfalls which have been known to make roofs collapse. In winter, you should wrap up warmly, as sub-zero temperatures are not uncommon. Many local inhabitants keep snow chains in their cars. The same can apply to Madrid and many a winter visitor from northern Europe has been caught shivering in a thin raincoat while the natives wear thick overcoats, gloves and scarves.

Avila

The ancient city of Avila is chiefly famed for its encircling walls. The walls were built in the eleventh century when King Alfonso VI conquered the city in 1085 and settled the land with people from the north. The walls are high with a perimeter of some 2,500 metres and include eighty-eight towers and nine well preserved gateways. Inside there are many ancient buildings including a pleasant PN where a good breakfast may be enjoyed in a large dining room. For other meals there is a good *à la carte* menu.

Avila is the highest provincial capital in Spanish territory, being 1,126 metres above mean sea level. Thus it often heads the list of cities with the lowest temperatures during the winter. This also applies to the summer when some visit to avoid the stifling heat of Madrid and enjoy sleeping under a blanket. The street market is held on Fridays, the cattle market on Tuesdays. Both are worth seeing.

Aranjuez

The river Tagus helps to cool the environment here. It flows through the grounds of the royal palaces to which the monarchy used to retire in summer. Aranjuez is worth visiting to admire the Royal taste, the extensive gardens and the town. There are plenty of shops and stalls which offer two famous local products (in season)—strawberries and asparagus. A special train runs from Madrid during which journey attractive hostesses in period dress will offer you free strawberries. On arrival the town band will greet you.

Alcalá de Henares

Roman remains abound in this city which was known then as Complutum. The city has recently been declared a national monument and is receiving a three million pound facelift, backed by EEC grants and aid. The city claims to have the longest under cover walkway in Spain, and boasts many ancient colleges and buildings. Its university was founded by Cardinal Cisneros in the sixteenth century and can be visited. Directly behind it is the luxury restaurant, Hostería, where Cervantes, the writer of Don Quixote, is said to have dined as a student. Cervantes was, in fact, born here and the register of his baptism has been carefully preserved and frequently reproduced.

You will find another sixteenth century relic here, the *Biblia Polyglota Complutense*. Cardinal Cisneros commissioned this Bible and it is in four languages. The first bride of Henry the Eighth (UK), Catalina de Aragón was born in this city as was Fernando I. The university thrived here until one fine day in 1836 it was moved to Madrid. After this the city (now some 150,000 in population) declined. It was hit badly during the Civil War but is now enjoying a renaissance and is well worth a trip. To get to Alcalá de Henares you should take the motorway to Barcelona and you will find it just past Barajas airport, 30 kms from Madrid.

The Hotel Bedel beside the old University building and Plaza de Cervantes makes a good place to stay or the more modern Hotel Topeca 40 near the station. In the *calle mayor* (main street) it is worth looking out for the Topeca cafe and restaurant. The restaurant is tucked away on the first floor, and reached by a corkscrew staircase. Attractive senoritas give excellent service and there is cuisine to match.

Guadalajara

The provincial capital of Guadalajara lies 30 kms further on towards Barcelona. Here the Palacio del Duque del Infantado is to be found. It used to belong to the powerful Mendoza family during the fifteenth, sixteenth and seventeenth centuries. References to the Mendozas occur frequently in history, among them many VIPs and land developers of the Americas. Also among them was that Cardinal Mendoza who had so many 'natural' sons and daughters that a special reception and fiesta would be given for them every two years. As a result of these Queen Isabel I of Castilla came to know his *bellos hijos* (beautiful children) who apparently ran into scores.

One of those *bellos hijos* was called Martin Gitano because his mother was a *gitana* (gypsy). He was the ancestor of that Miguel de Cervantes who, besides writing Don Quixote, had time to travel widely, distinguish himself in the naval battle of Lepanto when he lost an arm and spent many years as a Corsair prisoner in North Africa waiting for his ransom to be paid. This man was a writer, adventurer, traveller, poet, and playwright. He even died on the same day as Shakespeare . . . 23rd April 1616.

Chichón

The word *chichón* means a bruise in Spanish but there is nothing bruised about the appearance of this little village, famous for its central plaza where a weekly street market allows you to buy every type of fruit and vegetables as well as clothing and a variety of farmers' goods. Old houses with arched balconies ring the square. The balconies are used as grandstands when bullfights are held right in the centre of Chichón. Many houses have been converted into restaurants and bars as this is a popular day trip for the *Madrileños*. It is 50 kms from Alcalá de Henares on country roads and about 40 kms from central Madrid.

There is a passable PN with a large garden, fountains, pools, and numerous very productive fruit trees. This makes a pleasant, quiet day out and you can take home a bottle of anis liqueur or wine from the *Bodega Cooperativa San Roque* which produces wine with the Vina Galindo trademark.

Puerto de Navacerrada

This is Madrid's ski resort with one Nordic and twelve Alpine ski runs. Ski-able altitude is from 1,700 to 2,222 metres above sea level. All kinds of catering facilities are available from a thirty room hotel to a seventy five room hostel. All the necessary equipment may be hired *in situ*. In the cold winter of 1990-91 temperatures were sub-zero here for weeks on end.

It is a popular drive from Madrid and at times most of Madrid appears to be trying to park there, cars blocking the sole access from the south, the N-601. However, there is another access approached by taking the main highway to Burgos, the N-1, then turning left just past Lozoyuela, and taking the C-604 to Rascafría. At Rascafría there is a good *parador*-type hotel where you could stay. The road continues to the Valcotos ski station where there is ample space, or, if you prefer, you may continue to the crowded slopes of Navacerrada. Here the road peaks at 1,860 metres and then leads on to Segovia and the attractive summer palace of La Granja.

La Granja

Versailles will immediately come to mind when you enter the extensive gardens of this summer palace. That was the intention of its builder, Felipe V, the first Bourbon king of Spain (1683—1746) and the great grandson of Louis XIV of France. Terrace slopes rise upwards with elaborate fountains and watercourses. If you are very lucky you may arrive on one of the few days of the year when these are turned on. They are a kingly sight. The gardens are still used for State occasions.

The palace has some excellent sculptures and other works of art. At an altitude of 1,192 metres it provides a breath of coolness in the Spanish summer and makes the surrounding pine forest popular for picnics (*campos en el campo*) with many *Madrileños* and visitors who come from all over everywhere. When you tire of the palace, you may follow the road to Segovia with its fairytale palace.

Segovia

The name Segubia first appears in records of the second century BC, thus being established before the Roman legions marched in and built the aqueduct. The aqueduct continued to be used for its original purpose until the beginning of this century bearing witness to the quality of Roman engineering. Although modern traffic is having an adverse effect on its structure the aqueduct still stands and keeps the eyes of tourist cameras firmly focused on this impressive creation, half a mile long.

Nearby there are many restaurants specialising in the regional favourite of roast piglet. The roast lamb is very good too.

The Alcázar, Segovia's fairytale palace began life in the twelfth century and is, perhaps, Spain's most photographed castle. If you climb one of the corkscrew staircases to the upper watchtowers you will be rewarded with a view of *La Mujer Muerta* (The Dead Woman). This is a mountain range which resembled the body of a reclining woman with its two peaks, La Pinareja, 2,193m, and Oso, 2,192m.

Ríofrío

On the way back to Madrid by car you will pass this Sierra and the royal palace of Ríofrío which is housed in an attractive deer park. The deer come up to the car for bread and other offerings. The palace was built by the wife of Felipe V, Doña Isabel de Farnesto and was also the home of Alfonso XII. Besides the royal relics it contains an interesting display of regional fauna and flora.

Back to Madrid

The N-603 highway soon joins the *Carretera de La Coruña* which is usually crammed with traffic on Sunday evenings and evenings after holidays. A fine view may be obtained from the mountain pass called *El Alto de los Leones*, at 1,156 metres high but when the temperatures are sub-zero, its sharp gradients can be dangerous and it is better to take the toll tunnel. Guadarrama is the next village with a wide range of eating places, even take-away roast chicken. Then you can go straight back on the motorway—traffic permitting—to Madrid.

2
Dealing with the Spanish

Whether the differences in Spain are purely idiosyncratic or are the result of past history, they must be acknowledged. Some people maintain that 'Spain is just another country in modern Europe' but even a brief stay or study of Spanish philology will reveal that this is untrue and that there is no sign that this will change.

The European Community has started to bring the country in line with the eleven other member states but there is little sign of it actually happening. It was announced on entry, January 1st 1986, that there would be petrol filling stations of all types and all companies gracing the Spanish highways by 1990. These are still a rarity and there is every reason to believe this will remain the case—in spite of EC protests.

Since this is the prevailing attitude, this chapter attempts to tell you how to cope with it.

THE POST OFFICE

Most Spanish post offices from La Coruña to Tenerife open from 09.00 until 14.00, six days a week. Again according to EC plans, they should also be opening in the afternoons—but the old timetable continues.

The mysteries of the postal system—opening hours
Northern Europeans accustomed to drawing their pensions when-ever they please will find that 'morning only' is the general rule. As mentioned, opening hours are 09.00 until 14.00 with no overtime. During this period, you can buy stamps, collect mail from an apartado (PO Box), send telegrams, use the Post Office Savings Bank (*Caja de Ahorros*) and a few other things. However, that being said, woe betide you if you attempt to register a letter after 13.00, collect a parcel, or buy a postal order. In most post

offices this can only be done until 13.00, after which you have to wait until the next day.

Time is therefore restricted and the queues can make visiting the post office a time-consuming activity. If you have to collect a parcel, take a good book or use the time to brush up your Spanish as the queues may be very long. Standards have slipped back rapidly since Franco's time but the State has just promised to make an investment of 200,000 million pesetas during the 1990s. Nevertheless the public has become so accustomed to promises that it will take a great deal of evidence to convince it.

There are fewer mysteries in the main cities and the capitals of the provinces. Many postal services are available from 09.00 until 22.00 or even midnight. You can check out registered letters in Madrid's GPO all day, as well as check them in. Postal services come near to the European norm although you will still have to stand in one queue to buy stamps, another to register your letter, and yet a third if you would like the clerk to make up your parcel and seal it. (This is a cheap and welcome service which ensures that parcels comply with regulations). In some of the highly commercialised zones multi-lingual staff may be available—but they are the exception.

Please remember that these details are general, and there may be regional variations. If you travel from one part of Spain to another and you have important first class mail, it is better to find out what facilities are available beforehand rather than assume it will be the same as where you have come from.

Letters

Incoming and outgoing mail may pose many problems to the newcomer to Spain. The delays in delivering mail in normal residential districts have to be experienced to be believed so it is well worth obtaining a post office box or *apartado (de correos)*. It may save days on letter delivery and means that you can receive your mail almost as soon as it arrives at the local post office. This applies particularly if you decide to 'live out in the sticks'.

Bulky parcels of printed matter or other material will not be delivered to the house in any case, unless you happen to live in a big city in which case you may pay a special fee.

If you think you may need an *apartado* ask yourself the following questions:

● Do I receive a lot of mail?

- Could postal delays affect my income?

- Do I intend to live in an isolated location?

- Do I wish to receive letters as soon as possible?

- Do I receive cheques in the post?

An *apartado* costs very little and once obtained needs to be renewed annually.

Posting letters is also a problem. In the past the express letter (*urgente*) has been the solution. It cost 70 pesetas to send an internal letter, 80 pesetas for an international but those times are ending. For a time postal costs were pegged. Now the current express fee is 150 pesetas.

If your mail is not so urgent get into the habit of taking your mail to the nearest post office before 13.00. Although the official closing time is 14.00 most mailbags are sealed an hour earlier and normally only '*urgentes*' will catch the post after that time.

Special tips
- Use post boxes as little as possible and always mail from a post office.

- If you are anywhere near the main post office in a city or a town make use of its services.

- If you frequently have urgent mail to post it is worth going to the nearest airport which normally has a Post Office. Some indeed, have a special Post Office building well away from the terminals.

- Tipping. Formerly this was almost an obligation but is the exception these days. However, it is well worth cultivating the staff you deal with. A Christmas tip will be remembered all year and may even help cut out some of the queuing if you become a regular.

- Using the postal code will also help you to keep on good terms with the staff of *Correos* (GPO) even if at times they seem to ignore it. The Post Office publishes a cheap guide to postal codes which may also be obtained free of charge. It is called *Guia Codigo Postal* and lists each street in cities down to house numbers in small villages and hamlets. It is worth remembering that *apartado* codes end in 80, eg Apartado 14,762, 28080 Madrid. (This is the author's address.)

- Anyone who lives near the Rock of Gibraltar will tell you to post your letters in Gibraltar, if they are bound for Britain or the Rock. Vice versa also applies, so the Gibraltarians cross the frontier to use *Correos* for mail with a Spanish destination. The delays are considerable otherwise and it can take a month for mail to cross the frontier. It seems that *Correos* still remembers the time when the frontier was closed and people and mail had to travel via Tangier to and from the Rock. The special Gibraltar stamps are an added incentive to use the GPO there.

TELECOMMUNICATIONS

You have an important appointment with a VIP. Your car is trapped in one of the frequent traffic jams in a Spanish city. Fortunately—or so it seems—your agent's car has a mobile 'phone. No problem. A quick phone-call will let your VIP know you will be late. However, that is too obvious for Spain. You will find the lines hopelessly overloaded between 11.00 and 14.00 and you will receive a constant 'engaged' signal. From time to time a voice from the depths will tell you this fact in case you have overlooked it.

But do not panic. Punctuality has never been a Spanish virtue and Spaniards may even look down on you for it. The muttered excuse about traffic will be accepted universally, usually as valid.

Traffic jams have created an original service in Spain. Girls in brightly coloured uniforms circulate on foot among the cars in some of those streets affected and for a minimum of 200 or 300 pesetas, a driver may make phone-calls while trapped in his car to communicate his plight.

Telephones

Overladen telephone lines often slow business contacts. One British financier told me, 'Spain's development will be slowed by its inadequate telecommunications system'. In spite of an annual injection of billions of pesetas, there is still a waiting list of 400,000. Delays of several years are quite possible—although the waiting list can be bypassed if you are willing to pay. You will find it difficult to get a connection in most cities between 11.00 and 14.00 and in tourist areas in the evenings when cheap rates apply.

If you are on a business trip it is a good idea to make your telephone calls early from the hotel where you are staying. Working public telephones can be hard to find, and if you do find one there will probably be an impatient queue. Calls between 17.00 and 19.00 are likely to be the most productive, whether private or commercial.

Telefonica (the Spanish telephone company) is still a monopoly in spite of entry to the EEC. The most expensive rates apply from 08.00 until 14.00 and the cheapest from 22.00 until 08.00. This usually applies to internal calls, not international, but changes are possible now that the EEC are taking an interest.

The *Cia* (company) *Telefonica* provides the usual service numbers which are:

Enquiries	003 (provincial)
and reverse charge calls	009 (national)
	008 (international)
Repairs	002
Offices of the *Telefonica*	004
Time	093
Weather	094
News	095
Sports news	097
Others	098
Telegrams	522 20 00

To call Spain from Britain you should dial 010 34 followed by the appropriate code from the following list and the number of the person you want to contact.

Aguilas	68	Lorco	68
Albacete	67	Lugo	82
Alcira	6	Madrid	1
Alcoy	65	Mahon	71
Algeciras	56	Málaga	52
Alicante	65	Marbella	52
Almeria	51	Mérida	24
Avila	18	Murcia	68
Aviles	85	Orense	88
Badajoz	24	Oviedo	85
Badalona	3	Palencia	88

Barcelona	3	Palma de Mallorca	71
Benidorm	65	Pamplona	48
Bilbao	4	Pontevedra	86
Burgos	47	Reus	77
Cáceres	27	Sabadell	3
Cádizo	56	Sagunto	6
Cartagena	68	Salamanca	23
Castellón de la Plana	64	San Feliu de Llobregat	3
Ceuta	56	San Sebastián	43
Ciudad Real	26	Santa Cruz de Tenerife	22
Córdoba	57	Santander	42
Gandia	65	Santiago de Compostela	81
Gerona	72	Segovia	11
Gijón	85	Sevilla	54
Granada	58	Tarragona	77
Huelva	55	Tarrasa	3
Ibiza	71	Tenerife	22
Irún	43	Toledo	25
Jaen	53	Torremolinos	52
Jerez de la Frontera	56	Tortosa	77
La Coruña	81	Valencia	6
Las Palmas	28	Valladolid	83
León	87	Vigo	86
Lérida	73	Vitoria	45
Linares	53	Zamora	88
Logroño	41	Zaragoza	76

If you are making your call from Spain you may obtain the regional code by prefixing the regional code given above with 9. Thus Madrid, 1, becomes 91.

How to apply for a telephone installation

To do this you must submit the necessary forms which can be obtained from any office of the *Telefonica*. After that the wait begins. Since there are some 400,000 customers before you on the list it can be a trying experience. Delays of several years are still common. This is disastrous for any business. Fortunately many of the offices for sale or to let are advertised as having a telephone installed. Otherwise they would remain empty. As the same delays apply to domestic installations you should apply for a telephone as soon as you can.

To date, the only way of queue jumping has been to acquire a mobile car phone. This can be removed from the vehicle. It is often the only telephone available in some offices. It still costs a lot (about half a million pesetas) but apart from bribery this is the only way to speed up installation.

How to handle important calls

Suppose you are travelling off the beaten track. How can you make a phone-call? It can be difficult to find a public telephone let alone a working telephone, and even then it may be in a noisy bar. This is what you should do.

- Find a decent hotel. You will be.able to make your call in peace and quiet. It will, of course, cost a little more and a tip will be expected.

- Find one of the better restaurants or cafes. The same will apply as above.

- If you are in a city, look for a shop in the *Corte Ingles* chain of department stores. These all have a communication centre where you can make all kinds of calls in reasonably sound proof cabins.

- The offices of officialdom often have a public telephone hidden away.

- You can make long distance calls and reverse charges calls from any *Telefonica* office.

There are exceptions, of course. You may make calls from the Madrid GPO, but not from small post offices.

Fax and telex

Fax and telex units are normally available only in the main post offices of the main cities, and it would be a surprise to find them in provincial towns. In time this will change, but it is anybody's guess how long. Some private concerns offer these services, but they are generally very expensive, much above the rates charged by *Correos* and *Telefonica*. Incidentally, if you prepare a telex yourself you will be charged less if you take it to the main post office.

If you receive bad service ask for the *hoja de reclamaciones* (official complaints form). Normally the mere threat will be sufficient to settle matters but if you are intending to use the service regularly it is better to stop short of the actual deed. Just as a tip will smooth the way for you in the future, so filing a *hoja* will guarantee trouble.

Telegrams

This is one service you will find in most post offices but it is only available in the mornings when these establishments are open. During the rest of the day you may 'phone telegrams in. You are unlikely to find an English speaking telephone clerk, however unless you are in the Costa Blanca or the Islands.

Fax

This is different. When you want to send a fax you must fill in a form giving your name and address etc.

Some negative aspects

As post offices are open for so short a time you can buy stamps in normal shop hours from those shops officially licensed to sell tobacco, but not from the many other unofficial outlets for the weed.

Several years ago the EEC opined that post offices should have longer opening hours, but the traditional ways linger on. The hope was also expressed that services offered should at least begin to approach those available in the rest of Europe.

In the meantime the delivery of mail may take a very long time, fax transmissions are frequently very bad and telex lines over-crowded. Staff may be very unhelpful and unwilling even to try to understand a different language, let alone speak it. Complaints, when made, rarely have any effect.

WORKING HOURS AND HOLIDAYS

Banks

These have very similar opening hours to post offices. In summer, however, they may be closed on Saturday mornings.

The Administration

'*Nadie ama a su patria porque sea grande, sino porque es suyo*'.

Seneca. (Nobody loves his fatherland because it is large, only because it is his.)

This sums up the attitude of many officials, especially when dealing with foreigners. It was especially prevalent in Franco's regime and still exists to some extent even now. One favourite tactic is to make you queue. You may spend a very long time in one queue only to find you have been directed to the wrong queue and should have been waiting in the next one . . . and so on. Persistence is essential when dealing with the Administration and the one weapon which really pays off. The battle will be won when the Administration is made to realise that you are not going to give up.

As usual, there are exceptions. On the Costa del Sol, and the other areas where the influx of hundreds of thousands of foreign residents has raised the standard of living so considerably, you may expect better treatment. Just remember that in Spain a civil servant may be neither civil nor a servant.

Working hours

Offices are officially open to the public from 09.00 or 10.00 until 14.00. In practice this may be a little different. Spaniards are not noted for their punctuality so they may not arrive at work on time. Then it is the custom to have a cup of coffee. In this way opening hours may be curtailed.

In the Ministries the staff are supposed to work in the afternoons but if you telephone during this period you are likely to be told, '*Señor Tal y Tal* (So and So) is not back from lunch yet,' until about 18.00 when it will change to: 'It seems that *Señor Tal y Tal* will not be back this afternoon, you had better 'phone tomorrow morning'. If you are very lucky you will catch up with your *señor* somewhere in his arduous timetable and make an appointment.

Business hours

An infinite variety of office hours are to be found in Spain and any business traveller is well advised to find out in advance what office hours are kept by the firms he intends to visit. If this is not done a considerable amount of time may be wasted in fruitless visits going from one closed office to another.

The traditional working hours are 09.30 until 13.30 and 16.30 until 19.30, thus allowing a *siesta*. Nowadays there is a trend towards reducing the lunch break and finishing earlier. Multinationals, however, may insist on imposing Stateside or British working hours. Staff comment, 'We can make hardly any external contacts in the afternoons.'

In the hottest summer months Spanish companies may adopt the *horario intensivo* (non-stop timetable). This is popular with staff even though it means officially working non-stop from 08.00 or 09.00 until 15.00, five days a week. This leaves staff free to spend the afternoon in the swimming pool, or have a siesta, as well as giving them a free weekend. (In winter, banks and a surprising number of concerns work on Saturday mornings). It should be said, however, that the *horario intensivo* very often includes a meal break and the inevitable morning coffee.

Other variations
Another variable to be considered is the great regional difference in Spain, from the deserts in the Canary Islands and province of Almeria to the vegetation and climatic conditions of the north which can be similar to the British Isles. At the moment, however, there is a drought in the north and the deserts of Almeria are so green that Wild West films cannot be made there. This is thought to be due to global warming, but assuming that conditions return to normal you will find that business working hours are affected by the climate.

Some companies too are introducing flexible working hours.

Business lunches in Spain
The Spanish business lunch is one reason why an international survey states that Spanish executives waste about 40 percent of their time. They will meet at a four or five fork restaurant at about 14.00 and continue until 17.00 and later, and discuss business amongst many other topics. They may consume a four or five course meal and refuse dessert in favour of a strong coffee to fight off sleep and, perhaps clinch the deal.

Business trips
Spaniards like to show lavish hospitality. Any business trip for the top flight may include five star hotels and restaurants. Dinners may extend well into the small hours of the morning yet everyone will be bright and alert for a 07.00 start. Many Spaniards seem to be able to survive several days of this pace, with no apparent need for sleep—just a lot of black coffee. So if you are planning a business trip to Spain, you should arrive well rested and prepared

for a strenuous time during which luxury meals may well alternate
with factory and plant visits with little time for sleep.

Shopping hours

Those long Spanish shopping hours can fill your evenings if you
are an enthusiast for *compras* (buys). The main department stores
open from 10.00 until 20.00. Hypermarkets open from 10.00 until
22.00 and on Sunday mornings. The average shop will open from
09.00 until 20.00, closing for two to three hours around midday,
and even longer when the great heat arrives in summer. These
hours are the norm, subject to the usual regional variations.

It is extremely convenient to be able to shop whenever you like
in the same way as you can find somewhere to eat or drink. The
new *Jumbo* chain is opening a series of 24 hour shops and
restaurants in the main cities. Once you become accustomed to
these opening hours it becomes positively irksome to return to
northern Europe and find everything closed so much earlier. This
is definitely one of Spain's good points and there is no change in
sight.

Shopping outlets are supplemented by the street markets usually
held once a week. On this day the town will be closed to traffic
and the shoppers throng from 08.00 until 14.00. The market is a
colourful event and ranges in character from the cosmopolitan
atmosphere of the one in Javea (Alicante) to the typical rural
mercado in Asturias where bargains are still to be found.

When you go shopping, please remember the following advice.
It will save you a lot of trouble and expense:

- If you can, take a Spanish friend with you; if not, choose a
  shop where the prices are clearly marked.

- Shop around for the best bargain.

- If you need to replace anything, especially lightbulbs, it is
  always best to take the old one with you.

- Never forget to check your change.

- Keep a sharp eye on your money and credit cards.

Public holidays

These are a perfect example of clinging to established habits. Easter sees a massive yearly exodus, often to the same place. Christmas finds all at home eating roast lamb and *besugo* (sea bream) on Christmas Eve, a centuries old custom. New Year's Eve requires the provision of grapes. If you are to be lucky in the coming year you must eat a grape at each stroke of midnight. These customs are similar to many others around the world but the Spaniard is a great enthusiast for a public holiday. Fourteen of these are celebrated each year. Here is a list of the national holidays designated in 1990 and 1991. Those marked (a) have no fixed date, those marked (b) may be replaced by the autonomous regions for other celebrations.

	1990	1991
New Year's Day	1st January	1st January
The Holy Kings' Day(b)	6th January	6th January
St Joseph's Day(b)	19th March	19th March
Holy Thursday(a), (b)	12th April	28th March
Good Friday(a)	13th April	29th March
Labour Day	1st May	1st May
St James' Day(b)	25th July	25th July
Ascension Day	15th August	15th August
National Holiday	12th October	12th October
All Saints Day	1st November	1st November
Constitution Day	6th December	6th December
Immaculate Conception Day	8th December	8th December
Christmas Day	25th December	25th December

Puentes (bridges) and *viaductos* (viaducts) are famous and often condemned but are still celebrated. A *puente* occurs when a holiday falls on a Tuesday. Most people will also take Monday off as well to make a long weekend. Only a few unfortunates in banks or the odd office or factory where it has not been allowed will still be in work. *Puentes* are a way of life for the majority which cost industry billions every year. *Viaductos* are even better— or worse if you are an employer. These occur when a regional *fiesta* adjoins a national holiday for example 1st May is a national holiday and 2nd May a regional holiday in the province of Madrid. When these two holidays fall midweek people usually take the rest of the week off.

Regional holidays
In addition to all the national public holidays each of Spain's seventeen regions has its own *fiesta* and every town and village has another day for its own *fiesta*. Whenever the Government tries to

reduce the number of *fiestas* there is such a public outcry that the threat is never carried out. This permissiveness is doubtless a vote-catcher. In Spain obtaining votes has the same importance as a sacred rite in a pagan religion and the Spanish also take their holidays and *fiestas* very seriously.

Holiday shutdowns

Thus business visitors should make a check on holiday dates before embarking on any trip. Working hours are curtailed even more during main holiday periods. Spain virtually closes down during August, except for the main tourist zones. The inland cities and towns are virtually empty and it is easy to park the car. However many establishments will be closed and you may have a long walk just to buy a morning newspaper. Normal business contacts will be impossible as all those in positions of responsibility will be on holiday. It is also a very bad time of the year to fall ill and need hospital treatment.

Apart from the month of August itself 'anyone who is anyone' will disappear from the office between mid-July and mid-September. Business visits should be avoided during this period. Occasionally some Minister will give great publicity to the fact that it is his intention to work during August, but since the Socialists became secure in their majority, even this propaganda exercise is less frequent.

The same applies to the period between mid-December and mid-January. Since the official public holidays are 24th and 25th December and 1st and 6th January it makes a convenient break for the executive to enjoy a skiing break. The Catalans have another *fiesta* during this period, 26th December.

Working in Spain is often difficult, but during the periods mentioned it is downright impossible. Some multinationals have tried to alter the pattern but with little success. Any attempt to make the Spanish way of life conform to the European norm usually has as much success as King Canute with his oceanographic experiments.

VISAS

Permanencias

A visa is not necessary if you do not intend to spend more than three months in Spain. Even so, if you would like to stay longer once the three months are up you may obtain a *permanencia* which will allow you to stay another three months. You are allowed two *permanencias* a year although some police stations will only issue one.

To obtain a *permanencia* you must visit a police station which has a special department for dealing with foreigners. You will need your passport, three small photographs and a document from your Spanish bank confirming that you have a regular pension or that the balance of your account is greater than 250,000 pesetas. You should apply for a *permanencia* two weeks before the previous permit expires.

Entry Visas
It is illegal to stay in Spain for longer than three months unless you are a Spanish national, have a *permanencia* or a residence permit. If you wish to apply for a residence permit (*residencia*) you must have a visa. You can obtain an entry visa from any Spanish consulate or embassy and it should be processed immediately. In practice a consulate may refuse because you are not a national of the country in which the consulate is situated. You should apply for a visa about five or six days before you are due to leave as the three months begins on the visa's date of issue. If you apply at the Spanish Embassy in London for a visa you must have a full five or ten year passport.

RESIDENCIAS (RESIDENCE PERMITS)

If you are applying for a *residencia* for the first time you will need the following items:

● A current passport with visa.

● A certificate from the local British consulate stating that you are registered there.

● A certificate to show that you do not have a criminal record. (The consulate will usually provide this).

● A certificate of good conduct from the Spanish Ministry of Justice. This form is called the *Certificado de antecedentes penales* and you can buy it at the local tobacconist's (*tabacalera*). When you have completed it you should send it to Madrid.

- Four passport photographs.

- Evidence of means, such as a copy of a bank statement or payslip.

- Evidence that you have private health insurance in Spain.

- Proof of accommodation. This could be a rent contract or a copy of the *escritura* (house conveyance document).

- The tax stamps (*papel de estado*) which cost about 500 pesetas.

You may take these to the *Guardia Civil* yourself to obtain a certificate which must then be taken to the *Comisaria de Policia* or you may employ a *gestor*.

You must apply for a *residencia* 45 days before your visa expires. The first *residencia* usually lasts for two years, the second for five years. When you want to renew your *residencia* you should produce your income tax return, in addition.

ESPANA   VISADO

RESIDENCIA

VISADO pere una estancia en Espana hasta 90 dias con tres entradas y tres salidas. Expedido por C.G. (Consulado General) Londres sobre pasaporte numero B143254.

Fecha de expedicion:

* CADUCA A LOS 90 DIAS *

Fig. 6. Spanish visa. 'SPAIN VISA RESIDENCE PERMIT Visa for a stay in Spain of up to 90 days with three arrivals and three departures permitted in that time. Issued by the General Consulate in London against passport number B143254. Date of issue: . . . VALID FOR 90 DAYS ONLY.'

WORK PERMITS

Currently it is necessary to obtain a work permit if you want to work in Spain, but this may no longer apply from 1992 onwards. Before you can apply for a work permit you will need a *residencia*, or you can apply for a work permit at the same time as you apply for your *residencia*.

Restricted work permit

If you are considering working in Spain for a short time only it may be worth obtaining a restricted permit. This lasts for six months and may not be renewed. It has the advantage of being available immediately. A normal work permit will take anything up to a year to be processed.

Normal work permit

It may be necessary to employ a *gestor* (a person who specialises in dealing with paperwork) for this but in any case you will need:

● your passport

● certificate of registration with the British consulate

● a medical certificate

● an entry visa (unless you are staying for three months or less)

● two copies of your contract of employment

● seven small colour photographs

● a residence permit

A work permit lasts for five years. When you need to renew it you should have:

● the previous permit and two photocopies of it

● the residence permit and photocopy of it (unless the residence permit is part of the previous permit)

● your contract of employment and two copies of it

- your last tax declaration and two copies of it

- a certificate of good conduct from the local police and two copies of it

- seven small photographs

- social security forms C1 and C2 and two photocopies of each.

3
Buying Property in Spain

RESTRICTIONS ON PURCHASING PROPERTY

Since Franco's dictatorship and since Spain joined the EEC, restrictions on foreigners purchasing property have become less tight. Today the only restrictions that apply are the following:

- You must notify the Ministry of Commerce that you are purchasing property.

- You may not own more than three flats in the same building.

- You must obtain special permission from the Director General of Foreign Transactions if your building plot is greater than 5000 square metres (1.23 acres). This is viewed as a business activity even though you may only be intending to build a house for yourself.

CHOOSING WHERE TO LIVE

Spain is not like Chile, a long thin strip of land between the sea and the mountain ranges, and yet publicity has restricted the knowledge of millions of visitors to this topography. Spanish territory includes fascinating mountain regions with peaks of 3,000 metres, vast pine forests and every kind of terrain. So if you are considering a retirement home in Spain it is worthwhile giving some thought to the other possibilities before you automatically decide on a coastal region. After all, in Britain some people retire to the Cotswolds as well as to Sussex or Cornwall.

Some points to ponder
It is worth considering whether your dream home is to be used as

a permanent residence or a holiday home as well as deciding on its ideal characteristics.

If you need to know the climatic conditions of the seventeen regions of Spain you can write to the appropriate tourist office. It will detail with joy the large number of hours of sunshine but seldom mention very important features like the humidity.

Generally, however you should get out your map of Spain and ask yourself a few questions like the following:

- Exactly which type of climate would I most enjoy? Central Spain would be very suitable if you prefer a dry climate with very hot summers and cold winters.

- What are the advantages and disadvantages for me of living near the sea?

- Could I adapt to an island life? If so, the Balearics or the Canaries are obvious choices. Remember, however, that the Canaries are as far from Madrid as London and Majorca's airport is very crowded during the peak summer season.

- Is the allure of day after day of cloudless skies strong enough? It can become boring, believe it or not! It also restricts the conversation.

- Where do other people live? According to the World Health Organisation, Javea on the Costa Blanca is the most popular. Statistics show the greatest number of GB registered plates here than anywhere else in Spain.

These are just a few points to start you thinking but whichever of the seventeen regions you choose, you will normally find a warm welcome there. As you can see on the map, p. 10, the land mass is important. The mainland covers 491,205 square kms, and the island groups, 12,286 square kms. If you have a Greta Garbo complex and just like to be alone, then the sparsely populated wide open spaces of Spain's interior could be ideal for you. At the opposite extreme, those with a 'sardine tin' complex would be very happy on the beaches of Benidorm, Tossa de Mar or even those in the northern province of Santander. These northern beaches are becoming more popular now with the Spanish and foreigners as global warming continues to affect the climate.

Useful addresses

It can be very useful to write for information to those regions in which you are specially interested. Sometimes the information will even be supplied in English.

If you are intending to invest in Spain and/or establish anything from a small firm to a large company, the regional Minister of Industry would be delighted to hear from you. Many incentives are offered to foreign investors. Address your letter to the *Consejero de Comercio e Industria* followed by the address of the regional government in question. Each regional government has its own Council of Ministers (*Consejeros*) and Civil Service. Thus it can be no surprise to learn that there are now 2.4 million civil servants in Spain, counting all those employed by central, regional and municipal administrations. It all helps to explain why taxes are on the up and up.

The following list of addresses gives the name of the *comunidad autónoma* (autonomous region) first, followed by the title of its government and the address.

Comunidad Autónoma de Andalucía, Junta de Andalucía, calle Monsalves 8 y 10, 41001, Seville. Tel: (95) 421 88 60, telex: 72854.

Comunidad Autónoma de Aragón, Diputación de Aragón, Paseo María Agustin a/n, 50071 Zaragoza. Tels: (976) 43 14 61, 43 95 00, telex: 58008, fax: 43 58 49.

Comunidad Autónoma de Cantabria, (formerly Santander) *Diputación Regional de Cantabria*, calle Casimiro Sainz 4, 39003 Santander (Cantabria). Tels: (942) 21 50 00, 21 50 50.

Comunidad Autónoma de Castilla—La Mancha, Junta de Comunidades de Castilla—La Mancha, Palacio de Fuensalida, Plaza de Conde 2, 45002 Toledo. Tels: (925) 22 45 00, 21 16 62, telex: 47995.

Comunidad Autónoma de Castilla y León, Junta de Castilla y León, Carretera de Rueda km 3 5, 47071 Valladolid. Tel: (983) 41 11 00, telex: 26567.

Comunidad Autónoma de Cataluña, Generalitat de Cataluña, Palau de la Generalitat, Plaza de San Jaime s/n, 08002 Barcelona (Cataluña). Tels: (93) 302 47 00, 317 58 58, telex: 51545.

Comunidad Autónoma de Extremadura, Junta de Extremadura, calle
Jose Fernandez Lopez 18, 06800 Merida (Badajoz). Tels: (924) 30
49 48, 30 49 49, fax: (924) 30 12 03.

Comunidad Autónoma de Galicia, Junta de Galicia, Palacio de
Rojoy, 15705 Santiago de Compostela (La Coruña). Tels: (981) 56
60 00, 56 41 00, telex: 88097, fax: 56 38 60.

*Comunidad Autónoma de las Islas Balaeres, Gobierno de las Islas
Balaeres*, calle Marina 3—Consulado del Mar, 07012 Palma de
Mallorca (Mallorca). Tels: (971) 71 60 92, 71 26 04, fax: 71 16 53.

Comunidad Autónoma de las Islas Canarias, Gobierno Canario, Plaza
25 de Julio 1, 38004 Santa Cruz de Tenerife (Islas Canarias).

*Comunidad Autónoma de Madrid, Gobierno de la Comunidad de
Madrid*, Puerta del Sol 7, 28013 Madrid. Tels: (91) 521 45 15, 522
24 65.

Comunidad Autónoma del País Vasco, Gobierno Vasco, (Basque
Government) Palacio de Ajuna-Enea, 01007 Vitoria (Alava). Tels:
(945) 23 16 16, 24 77 00, telex: 35463.

Comunidad Autónoma de La Rioja, Consejo de Gobierno de La Rioja,
calle General Vara del Rey 3, 26002, Logroño. Tel: (941) 29 11
00.

Comunidad Autónoma de Valencia, Generalidad Valenciana, Palau
de la Generalitat, calle Caballeros 2, 46001 Valencia. Tels: (96)
3896 34 33, 386 34 37, telex: 63071.

Comunidad Floral de Navarra, Diputación Floral de Navarra, Avda
de San Ignacio 1, 31002 Pamplona (Navarra). Tels: (948) 22 72
00, 22 73 00, telex: 37817, fax: 22 76 73.

*Principado de Asturias, Consejo de Gobierno del Principado de
Asturias*, calle Suárez de la Riva, 33009 Oviedo (Asturias). Tels:
(985) 22 43 60, 22 40 63.

Región de Murcia, Consejo de Gobierno de Murcia, Palacio de San
Esteban, calle Acisco Diaz s/n, 30071 Murcia. Tels: (968) 29 20
11, 29 30 11, telex: 67641, fax: 29 24 06.

You could also try writing to the appropriate *Oficina de Turismo* or, if you prefer to impress, the *Consejero de Turismo* (Minister of Tourism). In some cases like the *Consejería de Turismo y Transportes* of the Canaries, and the *Junta de Extremadura* you will receive an attractive book which will give you plenty of information.

Reading the weekly English newspaper *Sur in English* will put you into the picture about all facets of life on the Costa del Sol, from clubs and scandal, to news and sport. Every winter there is a competition. The 25 winning couples are taken on a tour of Andalucía, enjoying luxury hotels and restaurants. If you are lucky enough to win, as we were, you will enjoy the experience.

The Canaries
The Canary Islands are the choice of many foreigners for a holiday home or something more permanent. The seven main islands and four smaller ones cover 7,501 square kms. They are 1,100 kms from Cádiz and are a mere 115 km from Fuerteventura to Cape Juby in Africa. Thus the climate and general appearance owe more to Africa than Europe. If you like the heat, year-round swimming and sun bathing—there are some naturist beaches—then the Canaries could be for you.

The tourist books talk of privileged climate. This means that they have a year-round season. The main flow of national visitors comes during the summer, and during the winter the Scandinavians flee here from their winter black-out.

However a stay on the islands is essential before you finally decide. Conversations with the locals may save you much expense. For example, although the guidebooks extol the constant warm climate the taxi drivers will tell you a slightly different story. 'When the *cálima* blows in from Africa, the heat and humidity become insupportable. Water shortages are frequent and serious drought periods which can be lengthy.' The *cálima* is a wind that blows in from Africa bearing sand from the Sahara.

Final advice
It is also a good idea to consider your chosen residence from the angle of winter as well as summer. What looks like a desirable residence in summer could turn out to have a leaky roof which drips water onto the beds. The unmade road leading up to it could become a quagmire in the winter rains. This applies everywhere throughout Spain.

You should also spend some time in the region and town of your choice. Perhaps you could rent a property there for a year, or several months at least before you take any practical steps toward a final move. When you have done all this you should have a clear idea of all its advantages and disadvantages.

There are in fact very few places to rent in Spain. Most people are owner-occupiers. When you do find a property to rent you should insist on a rent agreement.

TYPES OF PROPERTY AVAILABLE

The choice is enormous and ranges from the luxury villas of the millionaires on the Costa del Sol, Majorca and Costa Brava, to modest flats on the coasts of Valencia or Murcia where bargains may still be found.

Retirement homes

Catering for the retired and elderly is becoming big business in Spain as typified by the development called Almond Court at Muchamiel just 8 kms north of Alicante and 5 kms north of Alicante and 5 kms from its famous San Juan beach.

Phase One is mostly sold, Phase Two is under construction and Phases Three and Four will follow. It is an *urbanización* aimed at the retired. Many retired people from northern Europe are tempted here by the climate which offers 300 days of sunshine a year. The Manager at Almond Court, Senor Jorge Zanoletty Larrea, told me:

'About 70 per cent of our residents are British, followed by Dutch, Austrians, Italians, down to one German lady. We have designed everything for retired people, from a walk down ramp in the swimming pool, to a resident doctor and nurse, 24 hour emergency alarm service with call cords in each flat. As the third age reaches ninety and beyond, we cater for all their needs.

'We believe that smaller flats are better so these range from 45 to 90 square metres in the first phase, and in the second almost all from 60 to 80 square metres on average, with just one type of 126 square metres. In the second phase, the promotion prices are 7.9 million pesetas for a single bedroom flat, and from 10.5 million pesetas for a two bedroom unit. The location is only about 50 metres from the town centre, so near banks, restaurants, and in the mainstream—different from many *residencias* for old people in Spain which are isolated in the countryside. For every metre of living space we sell in a private flat there is another metre provided in community services with a social club, library, gymnasium, pool, washing machine area, and so on, including a restaurant and cafeteria. We also provide a meals service to the flats and numerous other details.'

The company which runs this scheme is known as *Inter-Spain SA*. It is 25 per cent owned by one of the main bank groups, BBV (*Banco Bilbao Vizcaya*), having a capital of 163 million pesetas. Other banks which give references are: *Banco de Alicante, Banco de Comercio* and the savings bank known as the *Caja de Ahorros de Valencia*. The entire project consists of 200 flats and apartments and the first phase was inaugurated on 15th November 1989. Ninety people live there now with spare flats available for visiting relatives. When Phase Two is completed there will be a small 24 room hotel for visiting relatives.

If you wish to buy one of the Almond Court development, you will usually have to pay 20 per cent of the total fee when you sign the contract, 20 per cent in monthly payments until completion of the building and the remainder when construction is finished but other loans are available. The Spanish equivalent of VAT, IVA, is payable on top of the purchase price.

The Almond Court scheme is interesting because it follows the example of many Stateside developments for older residents, and its services are likely to be extended. Phase Three is for more flats and apartments but Phase Four will be a nursing home for the elderly who require full time attention.

The Fisherman's Village
This a commoner development in all areas of Spain. It is exemplified by *La Alcazaba de Mijas*. This consists of offices, apartments and shops built in Mediterranean style and copying a fisherman's village, a welcome change from some of the horrible block developments which have ruined so much of the Spanish coastline. Similar attractive developments can be seen in Puerto de Mazarrón (Murcia), Javea (Alicante), the Costa Brava, and other Costas.

Luxury accommodation
For sun worshippers the Roca Llisa development on Ibiza is typical of many. Luxury houses are built into the rocks beside the sea. It lies between Santa Eulalia and Ibiza city and covers 200 hectares with a golf course and all amenities.

Some housing developments are constructed alongside or within

golf courses, some apartments in marinas and there are other
speciality complexes.

BUILDING STANDARDS

The standard of finished buildings in Spain is as variable as
Spanish geography. If you decide to buy a new property through
a foreign company the guarantee is usually good. The same applies
to a luxury villa in an *urbanización* in Javea or near Denia. But if
you have found a cut-price bargain flat in Almeria on the Costa
de la Luz, or in some *pueblo* in the *Comunidad Valenciano* then you
should exercise extreme caution.

Doubtless as time passes the EEC rules and regulations will come
into effect. For the moment the motto is, as with so many matters,
'money arranges everything'. If you buy a quality product it will
probably work out cheapest in the end. The bargain priced
properties may cost large amounts to bring up to standard and
your attempts to obtain satisfaction under the guarantee doomed
to failure since the legal system is so slow that the builder will have
disappeared by the time your case comes to court.

The best builders

In some areas with a large foreign population the state of the
building art has been bettered, usually by foreign builders who
have moved in. The product will be guaranteed to British Standards, DIN, or other regulations. For the newcomer to Spain there
is a lot to be said for dealing with these builders. Not only is the
language barrier ruled out, but such simple matters as kitchen table
heights, mirror positions, storage space and the like are provided
without having to embark on lengthy explanations. In Javea
(Alicante) Taylor is a well known builder and Country Properties
of Competa (Málaga) offer town houses, villas and others
from three million pesetas upwards. Advertisements on the Costa
del Sol frequently mention 'creative building services', 'German
Masterbuilder', 'ITS' (International Technical Services) and so
on.

On the spot

However, as stated before, there really is no substitute for local
knowledge which is impossible to include in any book in detail.
This can only be obtained by talking to people. They have the
experience and the latest information which can be invaluable to

you. A visit to a restaurant, cafe, bar or even a park may offer a golden opportunity to start a conversation on the subject closest to your heart, a property. Do not make your decision on the basis of one or two contacts or the over-friendly types who try to take you under their wing. When you have spoken to a dozen or score of people on the same subject and obtained a consensus of opinion, then you can come near to the truth.

The top-floor flat

Well over half the Spanish population lives in those large blocks of flats, apartments and duplex which are visible in all parts of Spanish territory from the population centres of the Canaries to Aragón, Galicia and Almeria. Common complaints are about the neighbour who arrives home in the small hours of the morning, the children who live in the flat above and who ruin your *siesta* and a long line of other all too common complaints.

Thus the choice of a top-floor flat seems obvious. But if you do buy one, please check the roof. If not, you could wake up in the middle of the night with as close an acquaintance with rainwater as Gene Kelly in his dancing years. You, however, will not be dancing with joy, but possibly with rage. The charming salesman who assured you that the roof was completely rain-proof will have moved on and you will be faced with a long fight to get the builder to waterproof the domestic cupola. Our battle lasted five years and we only achieved this through pure persistence.

The law requires the builder to issue a full guarantee of his work for the ten year period following construction but if it had not been for a constant barrage of letters, telephone calls, personal visits, registered letters, threats of legal action and general denunciation, we should have lost. Sheer persistence is a quality which pays off in Spain.

Of course, this is why many Spanish prefer a lower level flat or apartment.

NARROWING THE CHOICE

When you have decided roughly where you would like to live and what sort of property you would like to buy you should ask all those questions you would normally pose when buying property in any other country.

Is a motorway scheduled for the area? Is there any risk of a disco being installed nearby? These and many other questions may be resolved by paying a visit to the Town Hall (*Ayuntamiento*). As usual this may be time-consuming so arm yourself with a good book and a Spanish speaking acquaintance—except in the areas where foreigners are common. You may prefer to instruct your *abogado* (lawyer) to do this.

It is also a good idea to find out whether the local amenities are seasonal or available all year round. It might also be worth considering a property 'facing' the sun. Great heat savings may be made in winter.

You should also check the general condition of the property, especially if it is not new. Since rainfall may be rare in some areas of Spain under normal conditions, the assumption is often made that rain will never fall. You may see proof of this in the largest cities which flood regularly when there is a mere half hour of heavy rain.

Thus you ought to check that there is a damp-proof course (they are not always considered necessary). Floors may also be laid on bare soil and sewerage facilities should be checked in older properties.

You will meet many high-pressure salesmen in your property-buying efforts. Some will offer free flights from London and entertainment of various sorts. You should never sign any document when you deal with these types. Look for the 'soft sell' approach. It is often the sign of a quality product.

Nowadays it is very much a buyers' market so you may safely ignore such threats as, 'This is the last flat of this type that we have' and, 'It's the only house available in this area'. Today there is a wide choice of every type and size of property.

PURCHASE AND THE LAW

Once you have chosen your property, you should check its title since there are one or two nasty possibilities. Alternatively your *abogado* (lawyer) could do this.

● Registration. If you are buying a new property the builder will have to register it at the *Ayuntamiento*. This should be checked. Alternatively the registration of an older property should be checked against the *Registro de Propriedad* (property registry). If your intended property has no deeds, one of your first expenses may be to have the deeds drawn up.

- Tax arrears. If the owner has not paid certain taxes, the law allows a charge to be placed on the property. This will be recorded on the title. If you purchase such a property you will become liable for the arrears.

- It is perfectly legal in Spain for a builder or property owner to take out a mortgage (*hipoteca*) on the property you are interested in while you are negotiating its purchase or even after you have done so. If this occurs, you, again, will find yourself liable to repay the loan.

The Property Register (Registro de Propriedad)

Transfer of property ownership should always be registered though as usual in Spain this does not always occur. If there is any doubt about ownership it is wiser to abandon the purchase than engage in legal battles. However, in normal cases you will find this register useful because it will inform you whether the property has been registered, whether there are arrears of taxes or an outstanding mortgage, whether an agency or company is involved. It can be very complicated in the case of the latter.

The Property Register should be inspected twice. You should check it at the start of the purchase and again at the end just before you register your ownership of the property.

The legal process

Once you have done all this and transferred the purchase money into a Spanish bank in internal pesetas you will be ready to sign the conveyancing document (*escritura de compraventa*). No conveyance is legal or binding unless it has been signed in the presence of a notary. The notary will want to see a certificate from your bank to confirm that the purchase money has come from abroad and a copy of form TE 13, submitted to the Ministry of Commerce with the details of the purchase, approved with the official stamp.

Please bear in mind that the *escritura* is the only document which will guarantee your title. Any other kind of deed or contract you may be persuaded to sign will have little effect. Any legal redress may be a very, very long time coming.

Once the conveyance has been signed it should be sent to the *Registro de Propriedad* to be registered. Once this has been done (and in some areas it may take up to a year) your title becomes final.

The legal process described applies as much to the city as to the country and should be followed through carefully. The Spanish legal system is largely inoperative due to delays of many years and the *Tribunal Supreme* (Supreme Court) has a backlog of thirty-five thousand cases. Local courts may take five or ten years to get round to an average case. If you do not have a local to intervene, you might seriously have to take your life expectancy into account when contemplating legal action.

On the other hand, many thousands of foreigners have bought properties in Spain, followed all the legal processes and have had no problems whatsoever.

THE PROFESSIONALS

The Abogado
This man is a lawyer. You will employ him to safeguard your interests. This means that you must check that your chosen *abogado* is not already working for your vendor. It is quite legal for an *abogado* to do this, but it is obvious that there may be a conflict of interest. An *abogado* will give you advice, and take care of the legal aspects of buying a property. Needless to say he should be reliable. Some addresses are given at the back of this book.

The Notary
This man is a public official for whom there is no British equivalent. His duty is to ensure that legal transactions are carried out correctly. He has no interest in either party; he will neither act for you nor protect you.

The Gestor
You will obtain the services of a *gestor* from a *gestoria*. Again he has no British equivalent. He deals with all kinds of paperwork, licenses, permits, taxation etc.

ADDITIONAL EXPENSES

You may expect the following additional expenses on top of the purchase.

Tax on the transaction
If you are buying an older property you will have to pay 5½ per cent transfer tax *(impuesto sobre transmisiones)*. If you are buying from a developer you will have to pay 12 per cent IVA (the

equivalent of VAT) for a plot of land, 6 per cent for a private purchase.

Gestor, Abogado and Notary
The first two are obvious. The notary will charge a registration fee, and occasionally for his services (the vendor usually pays for these). The registration fee is calculated from the registered value of the property.

Rates
There are two sorts of rates payable: the town and country rates, and rates charged by local authorities for such services as sewerage. They are usually paid once a year between 15th September and 15th November but sometimes twice a year—depending on the area. Notification of payment due is not usually given and fines of 20 per cent of the amount due will be imposed if the rates are not paid on time. Thus if you are going to be away it may be worth getting a friend, or paying an agency, to take care of bills. If the bills are not paid the town hall (*Ayuntamiento*) can register a charge against the property.

In some areas surcharges on the rates are imposed. Although these have been declared illegal, the authorities have no policy for automatic refunds and it is up to the individual to reclaim the money.

Utilities
The Spanish are very strict in this area. You will receive bills every two months for electricity and water. If these are not paid promptly you will be cut off.

There are no gas mains in Spain. If you are intending to use gas you will have to buy bottled gas.

TROUBLESHOOTING

In the past, newcomers to Spain have been curiously trusting and indiscriminating when buying property. Whether due to a surfeit of sun or travel brochures, it has certainly cost a great many people a great deal of money. In fact you should exercise about ten times the normal amount of caution when buying anything, let alone property, in Spain.

This statement is borne out by the frequent publicity given to property scandals. These outrages are frequently perpetrated by foreigners on other foreigners. Edward McMillan-Scott, MEP, puts the number of Britons who have bought holiday homes at more than half a million. He has mail sacks filled with their complaints about every type of default in services not provided, incorrect descriptions, lack of planning permission, no basic services and so on.

International publicity given to the many existing property rackets fails to effect any sort of control although the EEC has begun to investigate. It may be of some comfort that even Spaniards get caught too. Two of the latest cases concern some fifty retired Spanish couples in San Sebastián who paid deposits of hundreds of millions of pesetas to a property developer who then left the country, and a flat in Torremolinos which was sold 23 times to different buyers.

If you would like to contact Edward McMillan-Scott you will find his address at the back of this book.

Another company designed to prevent people from becoming victims was formed by the Norwegian, Per Svensson, at the start of the 1980s. It is called the *Instituto de Propietarias Extranjeros* (Institute of Foreign Property Owners) and the address is at the back of the book. It was originally formed to review all the pitfalls involved in buying Spanish property.

Yet another organisation with the same aim is the Foreign Advice Bureau (FAB) in Torremolinos. It is manned by voluntary polyglot staff. As Señorita Rosa de la Prada, whose family founded the Bureau comments, 'In Spain, 85 per cent of offices, both official and private, speak only Spanish. So that immediately poses problems to many foreigners who do not master our language.' She herself speaks six languages and offers advice on a variety of subjects. Needless to say, this organisation is kept very busy so if you want to call in their offices, you should make an appointment. Again, you will find the address at the back of the book.

4
Driving in Spain

ACQUIRING A VEHICLE

If you choose to run a British registered car in Spain you must remember to keep it legally roadworthy in the United Kingdom. Otherwise the Spanish insurance will become invalid and the car will be illegal in Spain. This means that you must keep ready the car's latest MOT certificate and make sure that the UK road tax licence is displayed in the car.

Using your existing car

If you do not intend to stay in Spain for longer than six months at any one time, all you need is insurance. The insurance coverage available under EEC regulations is basic. If you want anything extra you will have to arrange it with your insurance company (and pay for it).

The main drawback to this scheme is that the car will be seized by Customs if you go over the six month limit and you may be unable to recover it.

On the other hand you could keep your car and change the number plates for Spanish ones. You would then be able to use the car while you are in Spain, but if you leave, the car can be sealed by Customs.

Making a tax-free export

You may choose to buy a new car in the United Kingdom (foreign or British make) and export it to Spain to avoid paying VAT in the United Kingdom. To do this you would have to buy the car direct from the manufacturer or sole agent and fill in Form VAT 411. The vendor will supply you with the form. You must then meet the following conditions:

- The car must be taken to Spain during the course of the next six months although you may use it in the United Kingdom during this time.

- Once you have taken the car abroad, it must stay there for a minimum of twelve months although you may bring it back for short periods.

- During this twelve month period the car is for your sole use.

If you do not comply with these conditions, even if someone steals your car and takes it to the United Kingdom, the Customs and Excise will seize your car and you will never be able to get it back. For this reason it may be wise, in that first year abroad, to insure the car to its tax-free value plus the amount of VAT payable.

However if you manage to get through all this without mishap, you may take your car home and sell it without incurring VAT at the end of the twelve months.

Importing your car
This can be an extremely time-consuming activity added to which it is almost impossible to determine how much must be paid in Customs and Excise duty and other taxes. It can be done if you have patience or a good *gestor*. There used to be a convenient Customs' loophole whereby you could deliberately allow your car to go over the legal time limit. The foreign owner would be fined and the vehicle seized and auctioned. The proceeds of the auction less the small fine would be given to the owner who had, of course, bought his car back. However, even in those days it depended on the good-will of the local Customs officer. In my case his wife was English.

If you do decide to import your car legally you will find leaflet V526 helpful. It can be obtained from your local Vehicle Licensing Office. You should complete Section 2 on the back of your Vehicle Registration Document and return it to the Vehicle Licensing Office who will provide you in return with a Certificate of Export, V561.

It is possible to avoid paying excise duty on your car if you have owned it for less than six months before you plan to leave for Spain. In that case you must sign a declaration at the Spanish Consulate in Britain or British Consulate in Spain that you are never going to return to the United Kingdom. You must also have proof that you have paid VAT on the car. The car will then be re-registered in Spain. You may not sell or transfer the car for twelve months afterwards.

Buying a Spanish car

This could save many of the headaches incurred by all the encounters with officialdom if you try to import a car.

Back in the 1960s, almost the only cars to be seen on Spanish roads were products of the SEAT factory in Barcelona, Fiat models 600 and 1500. Nowadays every type of car is seen. Many are produced in the huge auto plants in Aragón, Galicia, Valencia, Madrid, Barcelona, Pamplona and elsewhere. The multinationals export these cars to many countries. If you were to visit one of these auto plants you would see foreign quality control technicians conducting the final checks as rigorously as in their home country.

As there is no restriction on make of car these days you can choose from a huge selection. However, if you do buy a new car, you will be liable to IVA (the Spanish equivalent of VAT) at the higher rate of 28 per cent. A used car attracts 20 per cent IVA. This is higher than anywhere else in Europe.

If you want to avoid paying IVA, you may consider buying a tax- free car with tourist plates. During the first six months, special dealers will be only too pleased to do all the paperwork to provide you with a tax-free car. It does not have to be new. However you must pay in foreign currency and the normal hire purchase arrangements do not apply. You may get permission to run the car extended up to five years. Most companies which offer tax-free cars guarantee re-purchase, so if you are not likely to be staying in Spain for as long as five years, it is well worth considering this solution to the motoring problem. The paperwork may be handled at a *gestoria*. You will see many cars with special tourist plates.

There are disadvantages to this system, however. Tourist plates have to be renewed every six months and you will have to visit the *Jefatura de Tráfico* (the local government-run car administration service). It costs about 10,000 pesetas a year to use tourist plates and if you wish to leave the country for longer than two months you will have to get the plates sealed. When you return you will have to visit the Customs and the *Guardia Civil* to get the plates unsealed.

MINISTERIO DEL INTERIOR
JEFATURA PROVINCIAL DE TRAFICO

SOLICITUD DE CANJE DEL
PERMISO DE CONDUCCION

TASA 2.3

Profesional Núm.

Jefatura donde se solicita	Fecha presentación		
MADRID	*DATE*		*NUMBER OF*
D.N.I. *RESIDENCIA NUMBER*	Fecha de nacimiento *DATE OF BIRTH*	Clase de permiso *TYPE OF LICENCE*	Centro Reconocimiento Nº *MEDICAL TEST CENTRE.*
Primer apellido *FIRST SURNAME*			
Segundo apellido *SECOND SURNAME (NOT FOR BRITS etc.)*			
Nombre *FIRST NAME*			Sexo *HEMBRA - F VARON - M*
Domicilio Calle, plaza, etc *ADDRESS - STREET / SQUARE etc.*			Núm. *NUMBER*
Municipio *CITY / TOWN*		Pueblo *VILLAGE*	
Provincia *PROVINCE*			Código postal *POST CODE*

RECEIPT STAMP

(Validación mecánica)

DETAILS OF DATOS DEL PERMISO QUE DESEA CANJEAR *LICENCE TO CHANGE*

Clase de Permiso *TYPE OF LICENCE*	Fecha *DATE*	Núm. *NUMBER*
Organismo o País *COUNTRY*		

Codificación CR

DOCUMENTOS QUE SE ACOMPAÑAN

(Táchese con una X el cuadro de los que presenta)

1. D.N.I. y fotocopia del mismo. ☐
2. Informe de aptitud psicofísica, con fotografía igual a la señalada en el punto 3. ☐
3. Tres fotografías de 35 x 25 mm., con nombre, apellidos y núm. D.N.I. consignados al respaldo. ☐
4. .... ☐
5. .... ☐

VERIFICADOS LOS DATOS Y COMPRO-BADA LA DOCUMENTACION

Fecha ....
El funcionario.

El interesado, cuyos datos figuran en la parte superior, solicita el trámite que a continuación se indica (márquese con una X el recuadro del trámite que desea realizar).

☐ CANJE PERMISO CONDUCCION MILITAR

☒ CANJE PERMISO CONDUCCION EXTRANJERO
PUT X

LOCATION AND DATE..........
(Localidad y fecha)
FIRMA.

SIGNATURE

Mod. 2.40 (M. 28): IMPRESO GRATUITO

Fig. 7.   Application form for a Spanish driving licence.

JEFATURA PROVINCIAL DE TRAFICO

M A D R I D

DOCUMENTACION NECESARIA PARA EL CANJE DE UN PERMISO DE CONDUCIR
EXTRANJERO POR OTRO ESPAÑOL.

1- El solicitante deberá residir en Madrid.

2- Original y fotocopia del DNI o de la Tarjeta de Residencia.

3- Original y fotocopia del Pasaporte, con todas las entradas y
salidas.

4- Para españoles acreditar haberse dado de baja en el Consulado
Español, o si no lo hicieron, darse de baja en la Dirección
General de Asuntos Consulares del Ministerio de Asuntos Exte-
riores (Plaza de Santa Cruz).

5-Traducción oficial, expedida por el Real Automóvil Club de España (c/ José Abascal, 10). Están exentos de este requisito los
poseedores de permisos de conducción de países miembros de la
CEE.

6- Certificado médico psicotécnico expedido por un centro autori
zado. Están exentos de este requisito los poseedores de permi
sos de conducir de países miembros de la CEE.

7- El solicitante hará una declaración jurada donde se haga cons
tar la autenticidad ly.validez del permiso, así como que se
encuentra capacitado para conducir, con arreglo a las normas
de derecho interno.

8- Tres fotografías tamaño carnet.

9- Con toda esta documentación pasará por Caja para pagar la tasa
correspondiente.

10-A la vista de toda la documentación presentada, la Jefatura de
Tráfico podrá determinar la realización de un examen teórico,
práctico o de ambos.

Fig. 8.   Notes accompanying an application form
for a Spanish driving licence.

PROVINCIAL TRAFFIC AUTHORITY

MADRID
DOCUMENTATION REQUIRED FOR THE
(EXCHANGE OF A) FOREIGN DRIVING LICENCE
FOR A SPANISH ONE

1. The applicant should reside in Madrid (or whichever province applies; the example shown is the Madrid one).
2. The original and a photocopy of the *residencia* card.
3. Original and photocopy of the passport, with all the entry and exit stamps.
4. Applies to Spaniards only.
5. An official translation issued by the Real Automobile Club of Spain (calle José Abascal, 10, Madrid). Persons from EC countries do not have to supply this translation.
6. Medical certificate, which is issued by an official centre as described. However persons from EC countries do not have to provide this certificate.
7. The applicant makes a sworn statement concerning the validity of the driving licence, and that he/she is capable of driving correctly.
8. Three photographs of standard size (35 x 25mm).
9. With all this documentation, pay up, at the Caja (cash desk) with the fee. This is currently 1,540 pesetas.
10. After being presented with this documentation, the *Jefatura de Tráfico* will normally issue the licence required. In exceptional cases it may be necessary to take a written and/or practical driving test.

Fig. 9.   Explanatory notes accompanying the application form for a Spanish driving licence (see overleaf).

D. .... se responsabiliza
de la autenticidad y validez del permiso de conducir que se
pretende canjear y de su aptitud para conducir con arreglo a
las normas del Codigo de la Circulacion.

FIRMA .... MADRID .... FR ....

de .... de 199................

Fig. 10. Form for certifying the validity of your UK driving licence, as required
by the Madrid traffic department. 'Mr/Mrs .... accepts full
responsibility for the authenticity and validity of the driving licence presented
and for his/her ability to drive correctly and according to the Traffic Code.
SIGNED .... MADRID [day of ....
month/year].'

SPANISH REGISTERED NUMBER PLATES

The first letter denotes the province, or if two letters, the provincial
capital. This is to distinguish the provinces whose names begin
with the same letter. Then there are four numbers and two letters
(issued independently in each province) to indicate the age of the
car. Thus the latest registrations in Madrid are in the range:
M1234MD. You will find that most vehicles seem to remain in the
province of their origin except in holiday periods. Naturally trucks
are an exception.

If you would like to identify the cars you see on the roads the
list opposite will be useful. It could also provide the basis for a
game to amuse small children on a long journey.

There are 58 different vehicle registration letters in this list but
there are only 50 Spanish provinces. The other eight are one each
for the two North African enclaves of Spain (Ceuta and Melilla)
and the rest are state related: *Ejército de Tierra* (ET), the Army,
Fuerzas Aereas (EA) the Air Force, *Fuerzas Navales* (FN), the
Navy, *Ministerio de Obras Publicas* (MOP), Ministry of Public
Works, *Parque Guardia Civil* (PGC), to look out for, *Parque Movile
Ministerios* (PMM), Civil Service vehicles in general.

Matriculas Nacionales

Province etc	Letters	Province etc	Letters
Alava	VI	Lérida	L
Albacete	AB	Logroño	LO
Alicante	A	Lugo	LU
Almeria	AL	Madrid	M
Avila	AV	Málaga	MA
Badajoz	BA	Melilla	ML
Balaeres	PM	Minis. Obras. Pub.	MOP
Barcelona	BA	Murcia	MU
Burgos	BU	Navarra	NA
Cáceres	CC	Orense	OR
Cádiz	CA	Oviedo	O
Castellón	CS	Palencia	P
Ceuta	CE	Parque	PGC
Ciudad Real	CR	Parque Mov. Min.	PMM
Córdoba	CO	Pontevedra	PO
Coruña	C	Salamanca	SA
Cuenca	CU	Santander	S
Ejército de Tierra	ET	Segovia	SG
Fuerzas Aereas	EA	Sevilla	SE
Fuerzas Navales	FN	Soria	SO
Gerona	GE	Tarragona	T
Granada	GR	Tenerife	TF
Gran Canaria	GC	Teruel	TE
Guadalajara	GU	Toledo	TO
Guipúzcoa	SS	Valencia	V
Huelva	H	Valladolid	VA
Huesca	HU	Vizcaya	BI
Jaén	J	Zamora	ZA
León	LE	Zaragoza	ZB

If you buy a used car in Spain you should pay some attention to the registration plates and buy a car which has the same plates as that of the province where you are planning to live. If you do not, and buy, say, a car with a Zaragoza number plate and you live in or near Málaga, you will soon be known as 'the person from Zaragoza' even though you may be German, Norwegian or British. This may be annoying but is nothing compared to a car with a Vizcaya registration. Since Vizcaya is the terrorist region, such cars are very unpopular in the rest of Spain, and are more likely to be detained by the *Guardia Civil*. If you think you are on to an unusually good bargain with a used car, perhaps you should check that the number plate is not prefixed with BI.

YOUR DRIVING LICENCE

Since Spain entered the Common Market on 1st January 1986, the EC rules and regulations have begun to percolate into effect. Unfortunately there are still regional differences. If you meet a policeman in Zamora (north-west) Spain, he may have different ideas about what constitutes a legal driving licence from a polyglot policeman on the Costa del Sol. The former may wish to see an International Driving Permit and the latter would probably be quite happy with any current licence from an EC country.

However, as soon as you have obtained a *residencia* (residence permit) you should apply for a Spanish driving licence. This is issued by the *Ministerio del Interior, Jefatura de Tráfico*, and lasts for ten years if you are under 45, five years if you are between 45 and 70 and yearly after that. On the Costa del Sol you need only produce your *residencia* and foreign driving licence to receive a Spanish licence. In the more remote provinces it will need more paperwork and it may be best to employ a gestor unless you have a great deal of spare time and patience.

In the parts of Spain where foreigners are quite common, you may obtain your Spanish licence quite easily by yourself. All you need to do is go to the local *Jefatura Provincial de Tráfico* with the following documentation.

● Your passport, *residencia* and photocopies of each.

● Current British driving licence and photocopies of it.

- Colour photographs of yourself, measuring about 2.5cms by 3.5 cms.

- A medical certificate.

Medical certificates

At one time the medical certificate would be issued by the family doctor who performed some elementary tests. Now the tests have been brought up to EC standards and are carried out in special clinics.

These clinics are easy to find in towns and cities. They are usually clearly labelled, either *Centro de Reconocimento Médico para toda Clase de Permisos de Conducir* or *Centro de Reconocimentos Conductores y Armas todas las Categorias* (because hunters also have to be tested before they may obtain firearm licences and other documentation). They are open from 10.00 until 14.00 and 16.00 and 20.00 on weekdays and provide other treatments such as physiotherapy and saunas. Personnel in these clinics are normally friendly and cooperative.

The clinics are equipped with a full range of medical and electronic equipment to test your senses and reflexes and you cannot cheat. The medical normally takes half an hour and costs 2,700 pesetas if you are under 70. When you reach this venerable age and have to pass yearly medicals the price is reduced to 600 pesetas.

Once you have obtained your certificate of physical fitness you should have no difficulty in obtaining your pink Spanish *Permiso de Conducción* (driving licence).

Types of driving licence

Different types of licences are issued for different types of vehicle and are subject to different regulations. A B1 licence is issued to drivers of cars and vans up to 3.5 tonnes. An A1 or A2 licence is issued to motorbike riders and must be renewed every three years. A C licence is issued to truck drivers. A D licence is issued to bus drivers and an E licence to drivers of heavy vehicles with trailers.

You must carry your driving licence at all times whenever or wherever you drive on the public highways, even when clad in shorts. If you fail to do so a strict policeman may fine you—and not even a bikini will help!

If you lose your licence or it is stolen (and this happens to many foreigners) it is very easy to replace and will only take about half an hour in an off-peak period. You should go to the local *Jefatura de Tráfico*. The *Jefatura de Tráfico* handles all matters related to road transport, driving, car usage and ownership. It is usually filled with fast moving queues and there are 'No Smoking' signs which are fairly effective. See Illustrations 7 to 10, pp 67-70, for sample documentation needed to obtain a driving licence.

LEGAL REQUIREMENTS FOR DRIVERS

Spanish legislation is strict about the equipment and documentation that should be carried when you are driving. These are the items you must have before you make any trip:

• A complete set of spare light bulbs and tools for changing them if a bulb fails.

• The spare wheel should have the same pressure as the other four and you should have the tools necessary for changing a wheel.

• A warning red triangle with reflectors to put on the road if you have a puncture or breakdown, especially necessary on an *autovia*.

• All the documents relating to car ownership. If you take your car to a garage to be serviced you may also be asked for these.

• Up to date insurance coverage.

• Your driving licence.

You must have all of these when you travel. If the police should ever stop you, they will check every single item on this list.

ITV (Inspección Técnico de Vehiculos)
Any Spanish vehicle over ten years old must pass the equivalent of the British MOT every year. The test is called the ITV and costs 1,900 pesetas.

After the car has been tested you will receive a blue form listing all the possible faults. If the car has failed, the relevant sections of the blue form will be underlined and you have fifteen days to repair the car. If you can, you should get the examiner to write down for you exactly what needs to be done so that you can show it to the garage who will be repairing the vehicle. If you do not do this the garage may get over-enthusiastic and present you with an enormous bill for repairs.

Transferencia (transfer document)

If you buy a used Spanish car you should insist on receiving a *transferencia* from the vendor. The vendor should fill it in and the document will transfer ownership to you. The form itself is available from the *Jefatura de Tráfico*.

Municipal road tax

This ranges from 5,400 pesetas for cars under 12 hp to over 14,000 pesetas for cars with higher power ratings. It is normally paid between March and April and the *Ayuntamiento* should send you a reminder. However, if it gets lost in the post as 111,758 items did in 1989 according to the *Dirección General de Correos* you should pay regardless. If you do not, you will have to pay a 20 per cent surcharge on the bill. The tax itself is called the *Impuesto Municipal sobre la Circulación de Vehículos* and may be paid at the Council's tax collection office (*oficina municipal de impuestos*) if you can face an hour long wait in the queue. Otherwise you may send a postal order (*giro postal*), or bank order, or by getting the *gestoria* to deal with the matter.

The tax must be paid by all vehicles registered and used in Spain so it is very fair and compared with the car licence fee in other countries it is quite cheap.

Taxation is on the 'up and up' in Spain in all areas, and vehicles suffer as much as any so it is best to check.

Seat belts

Spanish legislation requires seatbelts to be worn in the country. When you drive out from a city, town or village you will see a large blue notice reminding you to buckle up. If you ignore it, you may be fined and as Spanish car insurance agents say that the average accident rate is two or three times as high in Spain than in France, it could also be a wise precaution. Every long weekend brings a death toll of between 50 and 100 on Spanish highways.

Don't drink and drive

All Stevie Wonder's exhortations on the subject are borne out by Spanish legislation. Breath tests may be carried out even when you have been driving perfectly correctly and there are heavy penalties for those who exceed the limit.

Lights

Obviously lights should be turned on at dusk or before, as you do not always notice the fading light. There are other circumstances, however when lights should be used and these are worth mentioning:

- when it is raining or snowing

- when you travel through a tunnel

- in underground car parks

You should not use lights when you park by the roadside at night.

MOTORWAY ROUTES

The main motorway routes which are toll roads go down the Mediterranean seaboard to Alicante. There is little delay in negotiating Valencia (which used to be such a bottle-neck). The motorways are being extended to Murcia and Cartagena and are planned to link up with Gibraltar, and eventually, maybe, even Africa, by spanning the Straits of Gibraltar with a wonderbridge or by tunnelling underneath.

The other main motorways are from Panadés, between Barcelona and Tarragona, and go north and west to Pamplona, Bilbao and Burgos with an extension under construction to Santander. Other isolated stretches exist in various parts of the country, see Illustration 11, p 76-7.

The A-6 starts north-west of Madrid and runs for 108 kms to Adanero on the La Coruña highway.

The A-4 links Seville with Cádiz running for 113 kms through flat country.

The A-66 avoids the Pass of Pajares, starting near León and ending after 77.5 kms near Oviedo in the foothills of the Cantábrica mountains.

The A-9, 74 kms long, links La Coruña with Santiago de Compostela. After that there are 57 kms of crowded main roads as far as Pontevedra and 28 kms of motorway to Vigo. Work on bridging the gap between Santiago and Pontevedra has begun but

Fig. 11. The Spanish motorway system.

it will be a long time before this section is completed since the topography is so difficult.

The Government is investing large amounts into its road construction plans in an effort to improve Spanish driving. *Autovias* (bypasses) are being constructed on all the radial routes from Madrid, the one from Madrid to Zaragoza being particularly welcome. These roads are toll-free and quite fast.

Much caution should be exercised, even on some main roads. Standards leave much to be desired. At Ateca and certain other black spots on the main road from Madrid to Zaragoza when two large trucks travelling in opposite directions meet, one will frequently have to back up for the other to pass. This is happening more and more often as more and more trucks pump goods country-wide into Spain.

DRIVING HAZARDS

Speed limits

So you have crossed the border with your car. Did you notice the speed limits? Normally, they are displayed clearly at every vehicle entry point into Spanish territory. The theory is as follows:

	kmph	mph
motorways which are toll roads (*autopistas*)	120	75
Autopistas with four or more lanes or three lane main roads and highways	100	62.5
Other main roads and inter-town connections	90	56.2
In population centres and where indicated	60	37.5

The practice is very different. Many Spanish drivers travel at speeds well over the legal limit. Many modern cars travel the *autopistas* and *autovias* at 150-160 kmph, while a few try to beat their personal best from A to B. Although the maximum speeding fine is 50,000 pesetas with confiscation of licence in bad cases, it does not seem much of a deterrent.

You may notice traffic lights in some towns and villages, especially in the north and west. If you are travelling at more than 60 kmph they will turn red automatically and are an effective means of enforcing speed limits. Shooting the lights, especially in the cities carries a heavier fine.

If you are caught you will be fined on the spot. If you choose to pay on the spot you will be allowed a 20 per cent reduction. If you do not, the fine will be sent to your home, by registered post, even as far as Scotland or Finland.

Beware if you spot a car by the roadside with PGC (*Policia Guardia Civil*) numberplates. It could be photographing speeding vehicles. The photograph is considered to be sufficient proof of speeding and you will be fined. Another more recent tactic is for one PGC car to be stationed at the start of a town or village and another to be stationed a mile or more down the road. The first car will radio details of offenders to the second car which will then stop the guilty parties. Unmarked police cars are also being used these days to take photographs.

You should also be warned that it no longer works to pretend to be an uncomprehending Englishman. These days it is 'pay up or else' and you will be handed a polyglot instruction sheet to help you understand.

Roadworks

These present one of the greatest driving dangers in Spain. One minute you may be bowling blissfully along a brand new *autovia* and the next, facing a bewildering array of multi-coloured traffic signs and lines on the road surface going all over the place. If you should be unfortunate enough to be experiencing heavy rain and on-coming traffic, it might just be better to make an overnight stop and start again in the morning when visibility will be better.

When you see the road works signs you should reduce speed and take it very easy. Then you should follow the yellow or orange lines painted on the road as they take priority over the normal white ones. Sometimes there will be several sets of lines and you will be very confused. That is why you should drive carefully to avoid accidents. Under these conditions you would never be able to win a court case if you have an accident.

Short cuts and delays

Map readers should be very wary of short cuts. Once off the main roads in Spain, you will find the standard falls to third world standards. Although you may save many kilometres in distance the trips will take hours longer and you may be exhausted afterwards.

For example, if you are driving from Garrucha or Mojacar in

Almeria to Granada and you are in a hurry, you should ignore the apparent short cut through Gérgal on the C-325. It took me an hour's rally driving to cover 33 kms on something that was little more than a mountain track. There was no traffic, just a continuous succession of tight curves. It would have been much quicker to stick to the main N-340 and N-324. Similarly from Jerez de la Frontera to Gibraltar. You should stick to the main N-340 again. It is quicker to travel from Madrid to Pamplona via Zaragoza than to try the shorter distance via Soria. The same applies from Lérida to Andorra. The parallel routes are definitely to be avoided.

It really depends whether you are prepared to sacrifice a good deal of time. The off-beat routes can be very attractive but the slow average speed in the mountainous zones of the southern Pyrenees, Santander, Asturias and Galicia has to be experienced to be believed. When time is of the essence the expense of the motorways becomes worthwhile. Other notoriously slow routes are the approach roads to Cuenca, and from Vínaroz (Castellón) to the mediaeval city of Morella.

Traffic signs
The most perilous of these is the triangular sign 'Give way to on-coming traffic', usually found at T junctions. Sometimes, however, it will be so placed that on-coming traffic may cut clean across your bows, the idea being that when one traffic flow has greater priority than another, the first may cross the road directly in front of the second. So if you see a large triangular sign at the roadside and another triangle painted on the road, watch out.

Flashing amber lights may mean that you are approaching roadworks, or that traffic lights are not working or even a police roadblock (often seen after a terrorist killing, or some other hazard). But the most dangerous signal of all is the green 'walk' signal at the end of the pedestrian phase of the traffic lights, because, unknown to the British pedestrian the drivers will be seeing a flashing amber light. Equally the unwary British driver will not be expecting pedestrians to cross as a matter of right. So special caution should be exercised around these lights.

Accidents
If you are unlucky enough to be involved in an accident, the *Guardia Civil* will soon arrive and take control. They are well used to dealing with drama and can be very helpful. They are usually very human people, anxious to help and very well trained and

equipped to do so. If a vehicle bearing the sign '*Atestado*' appears it means that the people in it are there to bear witness. The best attitude to adopt with all traffic policemen is that of complete cooperation. Belligerent comments may literally cost you dear.

Greatest danger

The greatest danger of all for the British is crossing the road. If you have never or hardly ever travelled outside the United Kingdom, you will be unaccustomed to looking left first before you cross the road.

Equally, once you have become accustomed to living in Spain, you will have to adapt to looking right before you cross the road on your trips back to the United Kingdom.

CAR THEFTS AND ROBBERY

Another source of annoyance to the car owner is the frequency of car theft. Many people leave their cars in the street overnight. In that case you should fit alarms, have your car windows engraved with the car's registration number, fit a steering lock and generally take as many precautions as you can. Perhaps the best tip when you are travelling is to leave the car in an overnight car park. Failing that you should park it under a working street lamp in a good neighbourhood.

Car radios disappear with great frequency in this country where every form of robbery has become a fine art. Removable radios are very popular. You will often see a group of friends in a bar, each with his car radio to hand. The modern locking radios may be useful or you could simply try to cover your radio in some way.

The usual method of stealing from cars is to use a number of steel balls on a chain to break a window. The radio will be seized and anything else of value that is in full view and then the thief will beat a hurried retreat. The long queues in the police stations (*comisarios*) to report stolen property bear witness to the size of the problem.

The latest most vexing habit is the custom of removing car insignia which fetch black market prices for use as keyrings.

USEFUL TIPS

Petrol stations

These can be very few and far between so it is a good practice to

ık topped up, especially if you are going off the beaten
her time to take special care is in winter when there are
The car heater could stop you from freezing to death if
ɩght in a snowdrift.

Some petrol stations give better measures than others. Campsa
has a good reputation, especially the self service pumps. When you
settle in Spain, you should conduct a market survey before deciding
on 'your' filling station.

Garages

As has been mentioned you cannot always trust these to carry out
the work you would like. It is a good idea to take along a Spanish
speaking companion. If, however, you are not satisfied with a
particular garage, shop around until you find one you can trust or
someone recommends one. Eventually, when you have been a
Spanish resident for a while the newness will wear off and you will
be treated more like a local.

Warning lights

Warning lights are used a great deal in Spain, especially on the
autovias and *autopistas* when an emergency halt may be very
dangerous with so many speeding drivers about.

It is worth remembering that if the *Guardia Civil* feel mean you
may be fined for neglecting to indicate after overtaking to bear
right as well as before this manoeuvre.

Bicycle races

If you see that one of these is planned, you should try to get away
from the route as soon as possible. Bicycles have right of way and
you may have to drive behind them for a long distance.

Roundabouts

These have the same legislation as in the United Kingdom, but
very often Spaniards do not obey the give-way rule.

Spanish drivers

These are not noted for their patience so try not to slow down too
much when rounding corners, and do not hesitate at the traffic
lights. Some drivers are prone to hit the indicators while talking
so be wary.

Some good points about Spanish driving

One welcome change is to find that Spanish truck drivers are some of the most considerate in the world. They will help you to overtake by warning you when there is an on-coming vehicle and they generally set a good example for their counterparts in other nations. They have a cooperative attitude that lightens the driving load on long trips.

Traffic signs are good in Spain although at times there may seem to be too many of them but they help to make for road safety. In Huelva, Zamora, Lugo, Asturias and Almeria they may not be as good as fanatics for the regional languages will deface them.

The traffic police (*Guardia Civil Tráfico*) too are good. They may turn up if you break down and give you the benefit of their mechanical knowledge. They are also skilled in first aid as they are often first at the scene of an accident. In some areas, they can summon a helicopter to fly accident victims to hospital—a major time-saving where there are secondary roads.

5
How to Stay Healthy

A HEALTHIER WAY OF LIFE

One of the best ways of improving your health is to adopt the Spanish way of life when you go to live in Spain. While many in the United States are going crazy over the 'new' Mediterranean diet the Spanish have been following it for centuries; cooking with olive oil, eating plenty of fruit and vegetables of all types, having wine with the midday meal and taking a *siesta*. Doctors now think all these increase your life expectancy. Even though the successful business man may not have time for a *siesta*, for those who do, like retired people and self-employed, it means that you can start the day anew every twelve hours.

If you share the Spanish way of life and eat with a Spanish family you will notice that fish and seafood of all kinds are frequently eaten in a huge variety of dishes. In fact, while the EC average for fish consumption is about 14 kgs a year per capita, in Spain it is closer to 30 kgs and used to be even higher. Doctors announce more and more of their discoveries which prove that fish, fish oils and other fishy elements can help you to a longer life.

The popularity of fish and seafood in Spain is borne out by visiting the numerous markets (*galerias*) to be found in all towns, large or small. You will find many fresh fish stalls. Hake is the most common type of fish, but nowadays you will find an increasing variety of other species, including salmon from Scandinavia and even Scotland at times. In the United Kingdom it is becoming increasingly difficult to find a fresh fish shop, but in Spain they are everywhere. There are also a great many frozen food stalls where seafood is sold in bulk. There should be no difficulty in producing attractive fish dishes as so many Spanish cookery books are being published.

Given the huge variety in Spanish cuisine and the house-proud

Bizcocho de Zanahorias

2 tazas de harina
2 cucharaditas de levadura
½ cucharadita de bicarbonato
2 cucharadites de canela
1 cucharadita de sal

4 huevos
2 tazas de azucar
1 taza de aceite vegetal (lo más suave posible)

3 tazas de zanahoria picada (muy pequeño)
½ taza de nueces picadas (muy pequeño)

Mezclar los ingredientes secos juntos; (en otro cacerola) mezclar el azucar, aceite y huevos (uno por uno); añadir los ingredientes secos poco a poco hasta que esté todo junto, entonces añadir las zanahorias y las nueces.

Meter al horno en un molde engrasado y enharinado unos 45 minutos, a una temperatura de 350° ó 400°.

Carrot Cake

2 cups of flour
2 teaspoons of baking powder
Half teaspoon of bicarbonate of soda
2 teaspoons of cinnamon
1 teaspoon salt

4 eggs
2 cups of sugar
1 cup of olive oil (low acidity)

3 cups of finely grated carrot
Half cup of walnuts, broken up fine

Mix all the dry ingredients together; in another saucepan, add the sugar and the oil. Add eggs one by one. Add the dry ingredients and lastly the carrots and nuts. Mix well.

Place in a greased, floured tin, and bake for about 45 minutes at 350°-400° F, 200°C, Gas Mark 4-5.

Fig. 12. A typical Spanish recipe. The word recipe from the Latin *recipere* meaning to take.

nature of many Spanish *amas de casa* (mistresses or literally bosses of the house) it is claimed that a different dish could be served at every meal for a whole year. This is feasible—but it might be expensive.

Many of the older housewives are glad to pass on their private recipes. These are often much better than those in the expensive cookery books. In exchange they could be interested in shepherd's pie, steak and kidney pie or other European recipes.

Thus you may receive a recipe from your neighbour like that in Illustration 12, p 85 'from Ana to Margarita, hoping it turns out well'. It turned out to be carrot cake—and very tasty too. If you find the translation of your recipe difficult you will probably find a friendly person to show you exactly what to do.

As well as swapping recipes and mixing with people, the *siesta* is important. It is described by Dr. A. Culebras-Fernandez as particularly beneficial to older people and working people, there being no harm in taking your daily quota of sleep in two doses instead of the northern European habit of just one. The sleeping requirements of an adult vary from between five and nine hours per day, so it is obvious that the Spanish need their *siesta* since they go to bed well after midnight and leave for work at 07.00 in the morning, bright and cheerful. Dr Culebras recommends a hour's *siesta* for people past forty. Churchill circumscribed his *siesta* to twenty minutes after acquiring the habit when he was a war correspondent in Cuba in 1898.

A relaxed attitude to life

This is most noticeable in southern Spain and weakens as you go northwards. Statistics show that cardiovascular deaths dropped in the 1980s in Spain and life expectancy increased from 72.3 years of age in 1970 to 76.4 years in 1985. This is above the European average of 74.4 and ahead of the United Kingdom, France and Germany. Infant mortality in the rest of Europe is lower only in Finland, Sweden and Switzerland. And as usual the ladies outlive the gentlemen.

PREVENTIVE MEDICINE

Spas (*balnearios*) are a very popular form of preventive medicine. They are often set in the most beautiful scenery like La Toja on a pine-covered island off the coast of Galicia, Panticosa in the

Pyrenees, San Juan de la Fontsanta in Majorca, Lanjarón, 50 kms from Màlaga and so on. They treat rheumatism, all types of digestive disorders and many other ailments, while helping to raise health standards and providing a leisure break from the stress and strain of modern business. The *balneario* habit is growing in Spain again after some years of decline, when it was considered old-fashioned. Now it has become very fashionable and many of them are being modernised.

The general set up for these *balnearios* is to have a main hotel with thermal baths and treatments from a hot spring with waters of medicinal properties. A full medical staff provides the treatment which may cost between a quarter and a half of a million pesetas for a ten day stay. However, there are usually cheaper hotels, *pensions* or lodgings nearby, so that treatment costs need not be as expensive. Many Spaniards are enthusiasts and go year after year convinced that their health is improved. The *balnearios* are also patronised by the French and some other nationalities.

There are about 100 of these establishments in Spanish territory ranging from a humble one or two star hostel to the five star luxury hotel of La Toja which was founded in the last century and is still the venue for many Spanish VIPs during the summer recess. They follow in the steps of the Romans who were some of the first to discover their benefits. An excellent map, *Mapa de Estaciones Termales, Balnearios*, is publishd by the *Secretaria General de Turismo*. If your local tourist office does not have a copy you could try writing to the head office in Madrid.

The map lists 59 *balnearios* showing their location and giving approximate distances from the nearest main towns. The full address of each is given, period when open (normally from June to September), the composition of the spring waters, treatments given, altitude, number of rooms and so on. They have five main regional associations who are glad to deal with queries and a national association ANET. The addresses are:

Asociación Nacional de Estaciones Termales (ANET), calle Martin de los Heros, 23-4° dcha B, 28008 Madrid. Tel: (91) 542 97 75, fax: 542 98 24.

Asociación Catalana de la Propiedad Balnearia, Paseo de Gracia 34-1°, 08007 Barcelona. Tel: (93) 317 03 12, fax: (93) 865 23 12.

Asociación Gallega de la Propiedad Balnearia, Hotel La Toja,

36991 Isla de la Toja, El Grove (Pontevedra). Tel: (986) 73 00 25, fax: (986) 73 12 01.

Asociación Balnearia, calle Balmes 191-5°-4/B, 08006 Barcelona. Tel: (93) 218 36 00, fax: (93) 217 10 95.

Asociación Valenciana de Estaciones Termales, calle Jesús 44-2°-3ª, 46007 Valencia. Tel: (96) 325 99 01.

Just within the Iberian Peninsula in the pocket principality of Andorra is the five star Hotel Roc Blanc which merits a special mention in the field of medicine. Skilled medical staff provide a complete geriatric programme using hot spring water and all the modern treatments to ensure that older folk feel youthful. This medical programme of rejuvenation is undertaken by doctors and fully qualified medical staff with many years of experience.

The Hotel Roc Blanc is situated in the centre of the largest town there, Les Escaldes, and nearby there are the best shops, stores and restaurants. A project is planned to make Les Escaldes itself a high class spa with complete thermal spring water treatments and others, with an investment of 4,000 million pesetas. It is already under way and will further augment the health facilities provided by the Hotel Roc Blanc.

NATURAL MEDICINES

The age-old herbal treatments and other natural medicines have become very popular in Spain during the last decade. Many of these treatments have the great advantage of no bad side-effects. In most towns and cities nowadays it is easy to find shops which supply products by Dr Vogel of Switzerland, whose books and natural medicines are known world-wide. Other Spanish concerns also supply special dietary foods and treatments. One of these is Prodiet which manufactures 300 products and claims that sales in 1989 increased by 30 per cent to reach 900 million pesetas. The main factory is in Igualada (Barcelona) with smaller ones in Vitoria (Alava) and Pinto (Madrid) and there is a nationwide distribution system.

If you would like to contact a naturalist doctor or herbalist you should ask in one of the shops. Some have consulting rooms, others will have contacts.

Treatments can be expensive but effective. As always it is wise to be cautious and ask the locals. There are quacks and fanatics in Spain, just as anywhere else.

The best doctors are those who have studied traditional medicine and branched out into this new/ancient art. They can inform you from both sides of medicine that pumpkin seeds may help cure prostate problems, porridge may help improve eyesight, that an instant cure for a persistent cough is to place a cold damp cloth on the nape of the neck.

If you are interested in other forms of natural medicine these may also be found. Foreign doctors, dentists and other professions are now permitted to practise in Spain under EEC regulations and they sometimes advertise in the many foreign language publications in Spain. Again the herbalist shops can help with the addresses of local practitioners.

THE SPANISH HEALTH SERVICE

A brief outline

The Spanish national health service is known as the *Seguridad Social* or *Insalud*. *Salud* means health and to quote a Spanish dictionary: *In, prefijo negativo* negative prefix. Literally *Insalud* means without health—a very apt term, since the National Health Service suffers from all the woes common to such services.

Regional variations are possible in *Insalud* as in everything else in Spain, but certainly doctors in the larger towns and cities see a surprisingly large number of patients in an hour. Figures of 20 or 30 people have been claimed in media reports.

There is usually a huge waiting list for hospital beds, 200,000 being the latest informed statistic. Reports are common of patients having died before a hospital bed becomes available. Many of the hospitals of the *Seguridad Social* are grossly overcrowded with patients in beds in the corridors. At times there are reports of rats, infections and other bad things. Thus it is far better to get your treatment from a private doctor or through private medical insurance.

These are not just bad impressions but daily comments made in all the Spanish news media. Nevertheless there are excellent doctors and specialists in the Spanish Health Service. The *Clinica Puerto Hierro* in Madrid has a worldwide reputation. The chief problem is how to get into the hospital.

Emergency treatments
One method of gate-crashing is to go to the Emergency Admission Department, which is maintained, as you would expect, for victims of road accidents, heart attacks and similar urgent cases. In case you hesitate to do this the latest report from *Insalud* maintains that only a third of the patients who go to this department (*Urgencias*) genuinely require emergency treatment.

If you are lucky enough to be treated by a doctor, you will receive first class treatment but there is every sign of the *Departmento de Urgencias* becoming snowed under with cases.

Services not supplied by Insalud
The *Seguridad Social* has always had the reputation for giving only basic coverage for medical and other needs, thus the only dental treatment available under its auspices is extraction of a rotten tooth. Glasses and other standard optical treatment are out, although cataract operations may be carried out if you meet the right doctor. Other subsidiary services are not provided either.

If you can, take advantage of all the medical services in your own country before you come to Spain. Visit your dentist, your optician etc. Otherwise if you decide on private treatment you could copy many Spanish people and cross the border for better or cheaper treatment. This applies particularly in the north of Spain where many go to France for dental treatment, which is much cheaper there. In the south many cross the border to Gibraltar for the same reason.

Those eligible for Insalud
If you are living and working in Spain you will have to make social security payments. If a secretary earns about £200 per week receiving her wages monthly, she will have to pay 6 per cent of her earnings. She will be issued with a nine digit social security number which gives her the right to free basic medical treatment, reductions in the cost of medicines, also unemployment and sick pay. The *Gestor* can help self-employed persons or in difficult cases. Normally you will find that your employer will deal with the paperwork. People who do not work in Spain can opt to join the social security system. Pensioners may receive the benefits of Spanish social security even while receiving their pension payments directly from their home country.

If you are British you should write to the DSS but you may expect a delay in reply of up to a year or even more. According to the DSS there is no problem in receiving your United Kingdom pension payments while living in Spain, but in case you decide to return to the United Kingdom it is better to continue to have your pension paid by the British authorities. Since many of the foreign language publications in Spain carry advertisements for property in their home countries it suggests that many return. The DSS has a number of helpful leaflets for those who wish to reside abroad, which cover paying reduced Class II payments to permit a full pension entitlement and medical treatment on the British National Health Service if you should return to the United Kingdom. Other alternatives are available.

PRIVATE INSURANCE SCHEMES

There are a large number of private schemes available in Spain, but it is very important to read the small print on the policies of the Spanish ones. Some of these will only provide coverage in your home town or in a certain hospital and additional payments may have to be made for specialist and other treatments. When buying private medical insurance it is advisable to choose a policy offering repatriation in serious cases. Here is a description of some of the schemes available.

Sanitas
This used to be one of the most popular private insurance companies in Spain and it provides reasonable treatment. Many Spaniards use this after having had frightening experiences with *Insalud*. Just recently, however, this society has changed owner-ship, as a result of which the fees have increased. This has led to considerable protest, but it is still an attractive policy and may seem reasonably priced compared with those in other European countries.

The Westminster Private Medical Clinic
This clinic is in Gibraltar and is popular with many of the Costa del Sol residents. It offers a medical which may last between 45 minutes and three hours, working on the premise that prevention is better than cure. When a cure is necessary, all the specialists are available and most of their fees may be claimed on most private health insurance schemes. This clinic's motto is 'British Health Care For You and Your Family' and this can be reassuring in a strange land.

Danmark AS International Health Insurance

This company advertises in the foreign language publications and offers a very full range of services to a high standard. Danmark is well known on the Costa del Sol and recommended by many there as giving prompt payment for expenses incurred by all types of medical treatment including the most serious. Many people feel happier with a foreign based company. This company has a representative office in Spain from which full details may be obtained.

BUPA International Lifeline

This company claims 'when it comes to overseas healthcare you'll find that BUPA goes to the ends of the earth to help'. It has special rates for people both below and over pensionable age. This company is recommended by many foreign residents and provides a complete service including repatriation if the case is serious enough. The initials stand for British United Provident Association.

Exeter Hospital Aid Society

This is another British company which aims to please and has a good reputation for its dealings with patients in Spain. Again it has a wide variety of policies available. Details of these may be obtained by writing to the UK address.

Other schemes

As there are so many foreign residents in Spain there are many Spanish schemes available. The locals will be able to tell you which are the best.

SPANISH HEALTH WARNING

One characteristic of medical services in Spain, especially those inland, is that August is a deadly month, literally. Statistics prove that many more die in this month than any other in the year. Why? The majority of doctors, specialists etc take a month's holiday during August leaving locums. Sometimes it is quite hard even to find a locum. So in all seriousness if you are smitten with a serious ailment in August you should consider seeking medical attention in another country. A book could be written on all the medical disasters known to have occurred in August in Spain.

6
How to Stay Wealthy

This chapter deals with the main everyday financial matters. A really complete guide to Spanish business and commercial matters would fill many volumes.

BANKING

Banks figure high on the list of any visitors to Spain. Apart from the traditional Spanish banks, an increasing number of foreign ones are moving into Spain. Lloyds, Barclays and others are to be seen more and more often. The main national banks are the Hispano-Americano, the BBV (Banco Bilbao Vizcaya), Santander, the Popular, the Central, the Banco Español de Credito, the Zaragozano and a large variety of savings banks united in one federation. All these offer normal banking services, but there are some differences. Whatever your plans, and however much you like Spain it is to be recommended that you do not close your UK bank account as the staff may be able to get results from your Spanish bank when you cannot.

Transfers

Spain and Portugal hold the record for the greatest delays in processing bank transfers in Europe. Thus, if you have to make a rapid transaction it may easily come unstuck even though you have the benefit of telex and other modern devices.

Once you have opened an account with a Spanish bank you can request your British bank to send the money direct but there may still be considerable delays. Somehow other banks will get involved and interfere. The best advice is to allow for delays when planning any transactions of this nature.

It is essential to have any transfer of capital or sums of importance fully documented. Nevertheless when the author was transferring capital from the United Kingdom to Spain to complete a property transaction, a large amount of money went missing. The money reappeared only when threats were made to call in the police.

If you are a newcomer to Spain you may well try to pay in foreign cheques to your Spanish bank. You will be told that these have to be presented at a branch of bank in the drawee's country. This may take a month or more so short cuts have to be found.

By the same token you may use these delays to your own advantage at times.

Normal Spanish bank usage

Any foreigner interested in opening a bank account in Spain is usually given a warm welcome and there are a wide range of services available. If you are acquiring a holiday home you can arrange for the bank to pay such accounts as the telephone, the electricity, the water, council rates and so on.

If you are a resident with plenty of time and a wish to keep an eye on the bills, you may pay the bills personally in cash into the appropriate utility's account at any bank branch. Personal attention may prevent you from paying the same bill twice like the time when *Telefonica* issued accounts twice for the same accounting period. The money was eventually refunded, but the amount of free credit must have run into many millions of pesetas.

However, since non-payment of bills may lead you into serious trouble it might be worth risking those standing orders, but checking the accounts carefully.

You will find that cheques are not used much in Spain. They are not accepted as a satisfactory method of payment by most hotels, garages, shops. Credit cards, however, are very popular and may be used for all sorts of shopping including the hypermarkets. Such cards as Visa, Access, Master Card, Eurocard and others are readily accepted against foreign accounts. This can be useful as your income may be paid into these and withdrawn as weekly shopping, petrol and other payments. Some supermarket chains produce their own credit cards, or rather security cards which means that they will accept a Spanish cheque, but only from known and trusted clients.

Some factors in your favour

These remarks apply to retired people, holiday-makers and the like, not business people.

Credit cards which enable cash to be withdrawn are used

universally in Spain. Cash dispensers may be found in most of the
Spanish banks and they will accept foreign cards. In some towns,
however, only one branch of a particular bank will accept them,
in others every branch will. It is certainly a fact that these machines
seem to function better if you request the Spanish instructions
instead of the German, English, French or whatever other language
may be offered. (The Banks will deny this).

Eurocheques

Eurocheques are a convenient method of paying for the weekly
shopping, the petrol and other everyday items. They have the
added advantage of taking a little time to be processed so that you
may enjoy one or several weeks of credit. It is therefore worth
finding out which bank takes the longest time to process Eurocheques. In general the savings banks (*cajas de ahorros*) are the
quickest.

Purchases with the Visa card may also take a fairly long time in
coming home to roost, another advantage in your favour. All
documentation should be kept for five years. This is a legal
requirement for Spanish taxation purposes.

Foreign banks

The approach of 1993 means that many restrictions on banking
practices are being phased out. Ex-property owners no longer pack
their suitcases full of bank-notes to take to Switzerland, or to send
by courier to other countries. Restrictions do still apply to taking
capital out of Spain so your bank should make proper records of
your capital to permit you to release it to another country if you
wish. Within the next year or two, the Spanish Administration will
have no authority over your capital and the Common Market
principles of free markets and free circulation of capital will be
enforced, spelling the end of these unfair restrictions. In the
meantime you should choose your bank carefully.

Credit Suisse could be the best bank for you with its excellent
service and secrecy. Branches exist in most countries in the world
and the most complicated instructions will be carried out reliably.
Credit Suisse have an affiliated branch in Andorra called Credit
Andorre. Again service is excellent and unlike most banks in other
countries any request will be carried out on the date specified.

Offshore banking

Andorra is determined to become an offshore banking centre—'but in its own particular manner, without copying any other centre, and seeing that it is an important part of our future,' the *Presidente* (CAP) of Andorra told me. All banks are represented in Andorra, local and foreign.

The Andorran banks have international recognition. Two are in the World Top 1000 Banks published by *The Banker*. In 771st place is Credit Andorre and in 986th place is the Banca International. They are founder members of the Andorran Banking Association which totals seven native banks, all anxious to help. The other banks are Cassany, Mora, Bacasa, La Caixa and the Banca Reig.

Gibraltar

As is well known, the Rock provides the foundation for many offshore banking services. It is even possible to form a private company there for a few hundred pounds and avoid death and inheritance taxes by buying your Spanish property in the company's name. Although the Spanish Tax Office (*Hacienda*) is making grumbling noises about this practice, assuring a future tax on property bought in this manner, it has yet to be passed and implemented.

At the moment Remington Knight Associates of the United States maintain it has the solution in forming a US corporation for the offshore company ownership of Spanish properties. Spain does not have a double-taxation avoidance treaty with the United States unlike Gibraltar and other tax-havens.

If you are interested in saving as much capital as you can, you will obtain many pointers by visiting Gibraltar, perusing its Press and the invaluable *Sur in English*.

INVESTMENT

Gibraltar is awash not only with many concerns anxious to help you invest your money, but also the inevitable scandals. Again the local Press will give many details but the locals themselves will be able to give you the best advice.

Spain has its own fair share of investment companies. These have become reduced in number since a watch-dog committee was formed a few years ago to monitor all transactions and especially those which offer a larger than normal profit margin. This committee is called the CNMV (*Comisión Nacional del Mercado des Valores*). It has to approve take-over bids, share deals and practices. The CNMV is presided over by an ex-Minister of Industry, Croissier, who has fined doubtful dealers many millions of pesetas, thus helping to maintain order.

EXCHANGE RATES

If you are planning to retire to Spain you should take full account of the fluctuations in the value of currencies. Some retired people have been forced to return to their home countries owing to this unpleasant surprise. You must choose a currency which is likely to maintain its international value. The Swiss franc heads the list, resisting the rise of the peseta against many currencies. The US dollar may be the worst having started at 60 pesetas each, rising to a peak of 220 pesetas each and now falling past the 100 peseta mark.

EVERYDAY SAFEGUARDS

Cheques
Whether you are retiring to Spain, work there or an occasional visitor, it is worth knowing the latest legislation concerning Spanish cheques (*talones*). The first line of a cheque must say '*por este cheque*'. An old *talón* without this phrase is invalid. The same applies to any cheque whose date is more than six months old. Post-dated cheques are paid on presentation. All dates must be written out in full in Spanish ie *diez de diciembre* not 10 de diciembre.

It is a common sight in Spanish banks to see people turned away because there is not sufficient in the account to cover the cheque, even though the law says that the bank must pay out whatever is left in the account.

If your cheque book is stolen you should inform your bank immediately so that your account may be frozen. As robbery is so common in Spain, many people carry only one cheque or perhaps two and hide away their cheque book at home.

If you make a cheque out to *al portador* it means the Bearer and the cheque may be cashed by anyone. So make sure it goes into your account and nobody else's.

THE SPANISH LETRA

Any consideration of finance would be incomplete without ex-plaining the *letra*, a word heard universally in Spain.

A *letra* is a form of hire purchase. It means if you buy a refrigerator and decide to pay a deposit of a third of its value and the rest on hire purchase you will have to sign maybe a dozen *letras* to the rest of the value agreed. You used to be able to complain about faulty goods by halting payment on the *letras* but as these days most people exchange the *letras* for a loan with a merchant bank or some other finance, the withholding of payments would not have the desired effect. In fact, if you do not have the funds available to cover the payment you may receive a *letra protestada* from your bank, forcing you to pay the amount and extra costs. This is a very common occurrence these days, so it does not cause the alarm it may have done fifty years ago.

One word of caution. If you sign a *letra* it becomes a personal debt. If you sign one for any concern make sure that concern becomes liable for the debt, otherwise you could find the debt of a housing development, cargo ship or car round your neck. This could be even more worrying than the *hipoteca* on property mentioned in Chapter 3.

FINAL POINTS TO PONDER

These are a few questions you should ask yourself if you are considering retirement in Spain.

- Is it worth forming an off-shore company in Gibraltar?

- Would a family trust based in Andorra suit my purposes better?

- Would Spanish or other national investment funds give the best results?

- How will currency fluctuations affect my plans?

- Which credit cards will suit me best in Spain?

- Can I adapt to Spanish cheque usage or lack of it?

- Would it be better to have my pension paid into a foreign bank and use Eurocheques to withdraw it?

- Which particular professional advisers should I choose?

7
How to Become Wise

This chapter aims to help you integrate with Spanish society by learning about the language, the education system, the social customs, the nature and culture of the people themselves.

EDUCATION

The Spanish have always recognised the value of a good education. Spain has some of the oldest established universities like the *Universidad Complutense* in Alcalá de Henares, founded in 1499. In those days graduation was celebrated in style: the results would be read to the general public in the forecourt of this university; those who had passed the examinations would be carried through the main entrance by their companions: those who had failed would be taken out through the back door, placed in a cart and conveyed round the town to be ridiculed. This university was also the first to admit women. Dona Maria Isidra Quintana Guzmán y de la Cerda graduated in 1785 and was nicknamed the Doctora de Alcalá.

These days education is taken just as seriously and the Spanish are usually prepared to make considerable sacrifices to ensure their children receive a proper education. Private education can be very expensive and is often run or controlled by the Catholic Church. State education is compulsory from the ages of 6 until 16 and is free.

However, as in so many countries at the moment, education is the subject of much discussion and new proposals. As yet it is not known to what extent the new proposals will affect Spanish education or even how far it has been implemented, Spain being the country it is. Since it is all rather vague the general principles of education as it used to be are outlined in this book and a diagram of the new proposals included. You are advised to check carefully with the Spanish Embassy Education Office in London or MEC (*Ministerio de Educación y Ciencias*) in Madrid.

Nursery education

In Spain both parents of a family often work and so there are a great number of private nursery schools. These establishments will take children from the age of 2 until 6 (school age). Arrangements are very flexible. These schools not only undertake various aspects of childcare, such as toilet training, but provide a certain amount of education.

Primary education

This is for children aged between 6 and 13 years of age. On leaving primary school there are two options depending on the child's success.

The *Título de Graduado Escolar* (school graduation certificate) is awarded to a successful student and guarantees entry to secondary school.

Students who fail to achieve this are awarded a *Certificado de Escolaridad* (school certificate) which allows them to attend vocational training establishments (*Centros de Formación Profesional*). There are three levels of training during which professional skills are acquired.

Secondary education (Bachillerato)

This lasts for three years while students are between the ages of 14 and 16. The successful child will be awarded a Matriculation Certificate (*Bachiller*) at the end of his studies. This qualification allows the child to take a university entrance course (*Curso de Orientación Universitario*) and take the entrance examination of the chosen university or to enter vocational training at the second level.

University Schools (Escuelas Universitarios) 1st Cycle

These offer three year courses leading to a graduate diploma or qualification as an engineering or architectural technician. Other courses available now are nursing, tourism, teaching, business studies. Once the student has this diploma and has completed a preparatory course, he or she can take a course in a faculty or higher technical school.

University Colleges (Colegios Universitarios) 2nd Cycle

The student takes the university entrance course in the first term of the academic year and then goes on to study in the relevant faculty.

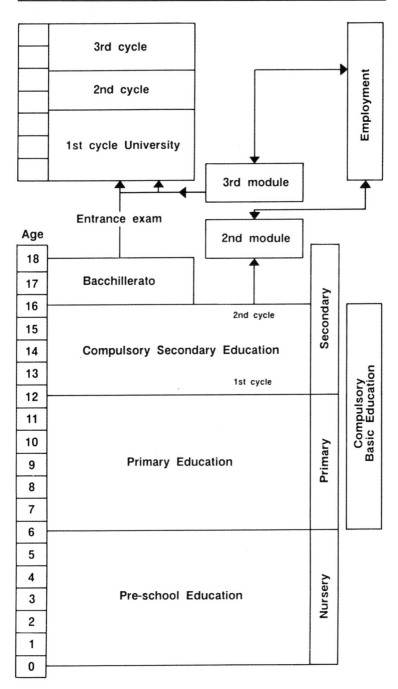

Fig. 13. Spain's proposed new education system (LOGSE)

Faculties (Facultades) and Higher Technical Schools (Escuelas Técnicas Superiores) 2nd Cycle

Arts and Sciences are studied in the faculties and engineering and architecture in the Higher Technical Schools. At the end of the five year course of study the successful student will be awarded the degree of Bachelor of Science/Art (*licienciatura*) or an equivalent qualification as engineer or architect.

Doctorate 3rd Cycle

The student has to submit a successful thesis after a period of post-graduate study and a considerable amount of original research.

LOGSE—THE NEW PROPOSALS

LOGSE stands for *Ley Organica de Ordención Géneral del Sistema Educativo* (Fundamental Law for the General Organisation of the Education System). It was passed on 3rd October 1990 and this is a brief summary of changes in general.

Private education is intended to run side by side with state eduction and enhance and augment it. Greater stress is being given to adult literacy and indeed education for all. Careers counselling is being introduced. Religion is no longer a mandatory subject; ethics will be taught instead to non-Catholics.

New universities are being established and new courses introduced. It is now possible to learn art, history, food science and technology, industrial design and there is greater stress on culture: ballet, theatre, painting etc.

Although educational experts were consulted, the introduction of LOGSE has not met with an enthusiastic response from teaching staff. Full implementation of LOGSE to the third stage of education is not planned until the end of the century.

Illustration 13, p 101, shows the planned proposals. It seems to indicate that the standard of basic education will be raised by extending the length of time a student attends school before the choice is made between *bachillerato* and vocational training.

Again it must be stressed that thorough checking must be carried out.

In general, however, foreign residents seem to avail themselves of nursery and primary education to a greater and lesser degree respectively. Young children easily pick up languages. Parents of older children usually prefer to make other arrangements for secondary education. This could be because it is so different from the British system. Spanish ministers and VIPs frequently send their children to foreign universities simply because the courses are so long in Spain.

LEARNING THE LANGUAGE

Adults are not immune to the process of education and it is recommended that you should attempt to learn *castellano* if you intend to reside in Spain for a considerable length of time. Many discover that the time and expense of a course in spoken Spanish proves a very sound investment. It will certainly enhance your enjoyment of Spain.

Castellano is a very easy language to learn because it is written phonetically. Once you have mastered the basic vowel and consonant sounds you will have no problems reading or writing Spanish. Many of the words share common roots with other European languages but the pronunciation may be a little different. Once you have learned the language a whole new world of communication will be open to you. Whatever their faults, the Spanish are never short of words. Here is a list of idioms, very useful to know and not always covered in language courses.

Useful Spanish Idioms

pegar la hebra	to have a long conversation
a bombo a platillo	with much display, ostentation
abrir calle	open a way through a crowd
a cosa hecha	certain to be done, a success
a cuerpo de rey	live like a king
a la vejez, viruelas	an old person behaving like a youngster
al grano	to the point, don't be vague
borrón y cuenta nueva	finish one subject and start another
cabeza de turco	scapegoat
como aguas de mayo	something very welcome
de Madrid al cielo	after Madrid, only heaven is better

diós los cria y ellos se juntan	Birds of a feather flock together
echar leña al fuego	Add new contention to a dispute
echar pestes	to pick a person to pieces
echar una cana al aire	Take time off, enjoy yourself, let your hair down
el gozo en un pozo	lose hope of fulfilling a desire
el saber no ocupar lugar	knowledge or education is always useful
es el cuento de nunca acabar	it's a long story
estar a dos velas	to be broke (financially)
esta sin blanca	to be broke (financially)
estar hecho un brazo de mar	to compliment a female on her appearance regardless of age
gato por liebre	To pass off inferior goods or services as high quality
haber gato encerrada	to have an ulterior motive
hablar por los codos	to talk non-stop
hacer pucheros	to weep like a small child
hallar la horma de su zapato	to find just what you want
hay más días que langanizas	there's plenty of time
hecha la ley, hecha la trampa	those who make the law also provide loopholes
ir con pies de plomo	to be very careful
ir de capa caída	on a downward path
loco de atar	really crazy, enough to be tied down
mandar a freir espárragos	to tell someone to get lost, jump in the lake
meter la pata	to put your foot in it

nadie diga de este aqua no beberé	don't say it won't happen to you
ni fu ni fa	(an expression of indifference)
no es santo de mi devoción	a person with whom one is not at ease
no llegar la sangre al río	the fight did not become serious
no se ganó Zamora en una hora	Rome wasn't built in a day
no tener donde caerse muerte	very poor
para muestra un botón	a small sample of the whole (bad) truth
pasar las de Caín	bad experience(s)
pedir peras al ormo	ask for the impossible
quedar compuesta y sin novio	to be left at the altar
sacar de quicio	to make someone wild, see red
salvarse por los pelos	escape by the skin of one's teeth
ser una cosa el pan nuestro de cada día	an everyday occurrence
subirselo a uno el pavo	to blush like a lobster
tal para cual	one as untrustworthy as the other
tener buen diente	to be a good eater, have a good appetite
tener el sarten por el mango	to be in the commanding position
tener mala pata	to have bad luck
tener malas pulgas	to have bad motives, disagreeable
tomar el pelo a uno	to pull one's leg
una de cal y otra de arena	one as good as the other is bad
ver las orejas al lobo	to see another's bad intentions
vivir de la sopa boba	live at someone else's expense

viva la Pepa!   to live without worrying about the cost,
to blazes with everyone else

If you can learn just a few of these, they will help you to integrate more quickly into the Spanish way of life, as does learning the language properly. It makes it easier for you to be accepted, even by those who are fluent in English.

Perhaps the only people who do not need to know any Spanish are the VIPs in multinational companies. They are surrounded by polyglot staff and are sheltered from the normal requirements of every day life. For them Spain is another step on the corporate career ladder, as they commute to and from HQ on transatlantic flights in the near stratosphere. However, for ordinary mortals who live at lower altitudes a working knowledge of *castellano* is a must.

Some foreigners live in ghettos with little or no contact with the natives. They are missing a great deal. You should take every opportunity to fraternise in a country where there is little racial feeling and foreigners are welcome.

Unfortunately, many do miss out on the delights of Spanish life. A recently published survey reports that some 70 per cent of foreigners are unable to maintain a normal conversation in Spanish. It is even more sad that over 20 per cent do not believe it necessary to learn Spanish. These people live in many of the *urbanizaciones* along the coasts. These have become foreign colonies and virtual ghettos. If you should wander into a cafe in one of these places and ask for *cafe con leche* the request may be ignored. If you ask for a *café au lait* or *reversée* you will receive quick service.

When you are buying a property it is a good idea to find out what nationalities predominate in the area. You will find learning Spanish considerably easier than Swedish if you want to understand your neighbours.

Spanish courses
You will have to decide which course suits you best. There is an endless variety. Some courses in schools are available on a national basis like Berlitz, Mangold, Assimil and so on. Many others are regional or confined to one city. Again the locals' knowledge will direct you to the best. All sorts of methods are available. One practical tip is to listen to the language as much as possible. Use the radio, play cassettes in your car. The sound structure will become familiar even if the meaning does not. Once you have

established a basic knowledge and you are living in Spain you will be able to appreciate many of the social customs.

SOCIAL CUSTOMS

Those who become acquainted with the basic social functions in Spain are showing real wisdom, even though there are regional variations as usual.

Births, deaths and other occasions

These usually involve four wheels and are regular get-togethers.

Baptism is a social occasion even for the most modern-minded mums and dads. First Communions usually take place in April and May, when the ten year olds are confirmed into the Catholic Church. There will be a real feast which will be paid for by even the most Socialist minded father.

At weddings the bride usually wears a long white gown. It is the opportunity for another feast with dancing and drinking lasting for many hours. A present is a social nicety, and a necessity for any close relative. Total participation will be required of you whatever your religious convictions. The customs of the Catholic Church still prevail even though only 20 per cent of Spaniards are practising Catholics. These celebrations are a costly business for the family.

Funerals are also an expensive affair. Bearing in mind the high death toll on the roads it is perhaps a wise precaution to obtain insurance to cover such costs.

When a friend or acquaintance makes his last journey it is considered a very serious omission if you do not go to pay your last respects or, to give it the correct Spanish term, *dar el pésame*. You must greet the family and friends by shaking hands with them all and saying that you are extremely sorry. You may say such things as 'I'm sorry *(Lo siento)*' or '*Les doy(damos) mi (nuestro) más sentido pésame*' or '*vengo (vengamos) a darles el*' or '*la (las) acompaño (acompanamos) en el sentimento*'. The words in brackets are used if you are not going on your own. The visible expression of grief is considered good form too, as is weeping in public, for many reasons.

Happy events

For those of us who believe firmly in the resurrection of Jesus Christ, his resurrection gives us hope of a future life, which helps in times of funerals and accidents. While grief should be publicly shown on these occasions, when Christmas comes it is a happy time for celebration over an extended period.

The family usually gathers together for Christmas Eve dinner with all the traditional trimmings of roast sea bream, roast lamb and all types of sea food, including king prawns and scampi and so on. A night of dancing and merry-making is traditional. Although this custom is dying out, if you have Spanish neighbours it is advisable to ask them what their plans are for Christmas Eve. It may be a case of 'if you can't beat them, join them'. The feast continues throughout Christmas Day, when you can wish everyone 'Feliz Navidad' (Happy Christmas).

The same applies to New Year's Eve. Gifts are exchanged on the Day of the Three Kings (los tres reyes), 6th January, or Epiphany. On this day there will be processions through the towns and cities with the Three Kings. Things are changing though; the most modern talk of Papa Noel and 25th December and give presents then. These are considered to be national customs, the regional ones are the fiestas which in the north consist typically of funfair entertainment, sports and competitions, dancing. Generally when you have seen a fiesta in Asturias, you have seen a fiesta in Galicia or Navarra or other regions. On the Mediterranean coast they will be traditional mock battles between Moors and Christians. In Andalucia they are religious festivals when the images are carried through the streets, or processions are made into the country to some small church (hermita). Generally a good time will be had by all, especially if some public weeping can be included. This is just as much an expression of happiness as of sadness in the real Spain.

LIVING WITH THE SPANISH

When your studies of language, local idioms and every day customs are progressing, you will start to get used to living with the Spanish and find that they are a friendly gregarious people who know how to make strangers feel at home. The family events are times when you can let your hair down and the local fiestas help you feel part of the scenery. Apart from these events there are family get togethers and ordinary invitations, all happy events. The social reserve which exists in other countries is almost unknown in Spain.

No class barriers
It is a common sight to see the workmen who are improving the pavement in front of a high class bar, having a drink on the house and being accepted quite naturally. They may not, of course, be quite so welcome at the golf club! Even in a five star hotel, you may use the wrong knife and fork without incurring the grim silence this would cause in countries nearer the North Pole.

Family life
Family life is still strong in Spain in various degrees. If you participate in it you may be surprised at the warmth which exists among family members. Wedding anniversaries and such events are well planned and the resulting conversation over the well cooked meal may last long after eating has finished. In the summer, many families like to go to special sites where fires can be lit so that the male members may show their proficiency in cooking *paella*, and maintaining the wood fire at the correct temperature. This makes a pleasant day in the countryside.

If you are contemplating marriage, you will doubtless have an able teacher to educate you in the customs but for retired people and others, it is useful to know that many families still operate as a unit. Even in modern families, parents are still respected. They may still expect their unmarried daughters to be home by 22.00 or 23.00 except in special cases.

Many families still have three or more children but the trend is towards two. It is also becoming more usual to plan a family rather than attempting to prove how *macho* the bridegroom is by producing a baby in the shortest possible time. In some cases it used to be 'just in time or born in the belfry'. This is rare these days since abortions though controversial have been made available.

Socialising
This can take many forms, from the brief invitation to have a drink in the local bar—where all the family is at home—to spending a day or the weekend in the country cottage/house/flat which is the extension of many a Spanish town house.

The late evening meal is well known. So if you are invited to dinner, the repast will probably start about 22.00 and finish at midnight, or an hour or two later if you are dining in a restaurant. Illustration 14, p 110 gives you an idea of the kind of menu you may expect at a restaurant.

La Antigua Cocina Mozárabe de Córdoba

EL SALMOREJO	750
LOS CARDOS CON ALMEJAS Y CAMBAS	1.350
EL REVUELTO DEL SIGLO XI	950
CAZUELA DE VERDURAS CON CORDERO	1.200
BERENGENAS CON PERDIZ A LA MANZANA	1.200
LA MERLUZA «AL ANDALUS»	1.500
EL RAPE CON PASAS DE CORINTO Y PIÑON	1.500
LA 1/2 PERDIZ «ZIRYAB»	900
EL CORDERO A LA MIEL	1.450
RIÑONADA DE CORDERO CON ALMENDRA PICADA Y PIMIENTA NEGRA	1.800
LOS ESCALOPINES CON SETAS AL ROMERO	900
SUSPIRO DE ALMANZOR	500
LAS DELICIAS DEL C. ROJO	500
HOJALDRE AL LIMON Y NARANJA . .	600

Las Entradas y Entremeses

JAMON SERRANO	1.500
CAÑA DE LOMO DE JABUGO	1.300
SALMON AHUMADO «NORUEGO» . . .	1.600
ENSALADA DE SALMON Y ANGULAS	2.200
SURTIDO DE AHUMADOS	1.500
BONITO DE BERMEO ENCEBOLLADO CON PIMIENTOS AL SARMIENTO . . .	950
ESPARRAGOS FRIOS DOS SALSAS . .	850
ENSALADA ANDALUZA	475
SALMON MARINADO AL CULANTRO	1.600
MUSSE DE ESPARRAGOS AL APIO . .	750
QUESO MANCHEGO AÑEJO CURADO EN ACEITE	650

I.V.A. NO INCLUIDO

Las Sopas

EL GAZPACHO DE ALMENDRAS   700

EL GAZPACHO CORDOBES   600

LA SOPA DEL MAR   900

LA SOPA DE CAMPIÑA A LA
HIERBABUENA CON JAMON   750

Las Verduras

NUESTRO REVUELTO   900

ALCACHOFAS A LA
MONTILLANA   850

LOS PIMIENTOS DEL PIQUILLO
RELLENOS CON MARISCOS Y
PESCADO 1.050

Aves y Caza

CONEJO EN PEPITORIA   850

MUSLOS DE CAPON RELLENOS
AL FOIE-GRAS   950

LA PERDIZ ENCEBOLLADA 1.650

MAGRET DE OCA 1.700

Los Pescados

EL PEZ DE ESPADA
AL HORNO   900

LOMOS DE MERLUZA CANTABRICA
CON ANGULAS 2.200

CAZUELA DE PESCADO AL
PEDRO XIMENEZ 1.500

LENGUADO AL VINAGRE BLANCO
(S/ mercado y peso) ....

EL RAPE CON SALMON AHUMADO
EN SALSA VERDE 1.950

SALMON FRESCO AL VINO
DEL DUERO 1.700

Las Carnes

RABOS DE TORO A MI ESTILO   975

ENTRECOT DE CEBON 1.600

LAS CHULETAS DE CORDERO 1.450

EL SOLOMILLO A LA PARRILLA 1.500

LA PIERNA DE CORDERO
AL HORNO 1.500

CHULETAS DE LALIN 1.750

Los Vinos de la Casa

VALDEPEÑAS   450

VEGA DEL DUERO 83 ....   1.300

Cardenal Herrero, 28. Telfs.: 47 53 75 - 47 80 01 - 14003 Córdoba

Fig. 14. Sample Spanish restaurant menu.

It is also the pleasant custom for the entire family to be present at the table, youngest to oldest. Conversation is usually loud and sustained, no awkward British silences. You may almost have to shout to get a comment in at the right moment. The Spaniards are expert at talking and eating at the same time. Both are enjoyed and taken seriously as arts to be mastered, an essential part of one's education.

Etiquette
If you intend staying with a Spanish family remember

- Breakfast will usually be light, lunch and dinner/supper plentiful.

- A mid-morning snack or mid-afternoon tea (*merienda*) is often served. This will help tide you over until the next proper meal.

- Hospitality may be expansive. If you are invited to a family feast it is bad form not to enjoy it to the full.

- Special occasions result in special meals, and, again, the host will be offended if you do not partake of every dish.

Family feasts may include hors d'oeuvres, soup, fish, meat and a dessert. However, if you are eating *merienda*, dish after dish of delicacies may appear, all to be sampled and enjoyed.

Please remember that it is the custom for any guest or guests to take a gift for the *creatora* of the coming repast. This may be flowers or more normally a kilo of *pasteles* (small cakes) which everyone may enjoy with the coffee at the end of the meal. A bottle of good wine also makes an acceptable gift. Illustration 15 p 113 will help you choose a suitable wine.

If you have Spanish neighbours you may invite them for coffee, then perhaps *merienda* and later, meals or outings if you become really friendly. There is little resistance to foreigners except in the most isolated parts of Spain. On the Costa del Sol, Majorca and parts of the Canaries the importance of foreigners in raising living standards is fully appreciated and you should be made to feel welcome. The mayors (*alcaldes*) of some towns make special arrangements for residents who are natives of other countries.

Fig. 15. Vintage wine guide.

Tapas

These have become so well known that books have been written
on the subject and bars named after them. This excellent Spanish
custom is now becoming international. For newcomers to Spain,
tapas are delicious morsels of all sorts of delicacies. They are served
during the lunch hour as an accompaniment to the drinks you may
order before having lunch. Originally *tapas* were pieces of highly
spiced sausage (*chorizo*) served with a *copito* (small glass) of wine.
These days an extensive range of goodies is on offer. This is one
of the many pleasant features of Spain which may be enjoyed by
the whole family on their Sunday outing.

After *tapas* the typical family returns to a hearty lunch so if you
have been invited along it is as well not to have eaten too many
tapas.

Lunch-time Tertulias

There is no danger of a spider attack if you are invited to one of
these. It is a daily meeting of old friends in their favourite cafe.
Current topics will be discussed in a friendly atmosphere. In the
upper class restaurants of Madrid's *calle de Alcalá* in León, it takes
on the appearance of a traditional ceremony. Special tables are
reserved for the same (normally) select group every day. The
permanent nature of these *tertulias* in the same cafe at the same
table with the same participants underlines a characteristic of many

Spaniards, the love of tradition and retention of old habits. Although it may be the 'in thing' to be an atheistic politician, a Spaniard would probably never dream of allowing his child to remain unbaptised. The same is true of holidays. Many families own and return year after year to the same flat or chalet in a particular seaside resort.

Wine
You will find vineyards in almost every part of Spain, except the most humid. Wine has long been glorified in Spanish literature, exported in billions of litres and enjoyed by millions of tourists as well as the Spanish themselves. Curiously enough, although wine can be bought almost anywhere at any time, drunken behaviour is less frequently seen in public than in those countries where the purchase of wine is restricted. This does not mean that there are no alcoholics in Spain. Alcoholism is often described as a major problem, but it applies also to the foreign population. On the Costa del Sol, the 'sun-downer' is often followed by the 'sun-riser' and continues through the day and night.

Good wine should never be abused, however, and there are plenty of good wines as you can see from Illustration 15 p 113. If you look at it you will see that 1982 is considered to be a top year for Rioja and 1972 the worst. 1981, 1984 and 1989 are good years for Valdepenas. Wine may also be a good investment.

THE SPANISH CHARACTER

It is difficult to write about the 'typical' Spaniard, considering all the regional differences and the great changes that have taken place over the last twenty to thirty years. The younger generation have become more and more preoccupied with the material offerings of life. They may spend up to the very last peseta, meaning a considerable combined income in many modern marriages. At Christmas the couples may be several pay cheques ahead of their actual income with credit cards stretched to the limit.

Amando de Miguel observes in his book *Los Españoles: 'Quéde-monos como somos, un pueblo viejo, teatrero, tierno, socarrón y alboretador'*. (We remain as we are, a people who have ancient roots, and are theatrical, tender in feelings, ironical and boisterous). After a five course luncheon in a five star restaurant where you may have had to shout to make yourself heard across the table, you may feel the last adjective could be put more forcibly. In fact, *alboretador* may be translated as noisy, turbulent, rebellious or mischief-making. All of these describe the Spanish character and you should take it into account in your dealings with them.

Señor don Julio Caro-Baroja, a Spanish historian, linguist and anthropologist, opines, 'I have always believed that a Spaniard is not an individualist, but a *personalist*, which is different. He is a man who concentrates so much on himself, that he only knows about himself. At the same time, his impetus is such that it seems that no one else exists, in a way which is frightening.' This argument is used by some people to explain why a driver may not use his indicators—everyone should know where he is going!

Some traits and trends

In spite of the faults in the Spanish character in general, *extremismo, celos o enviadia* (jealousy or envy), the saving grace of the Spanish is their gregariousness and hospitality.

The hospitality is open-hearted and even excessive. The discussion over who should pay the bill for a round of drinks can be heated. Each side claims his right to pay—so unlike other countries.

The cafe habit is firmly implanted in Spain. Most people have a favourite place for morning coffee, lunches out, evening meals and so on. That place becomes a kind of extension to the home. The entire family will be there from the very youngest to the very oldest. Conversations may go on way past midnight in the summer and, as mentioned, there will be little sign of drunkenness.

It is difficult to be lonely in Spain. If you stop to cross the road, a stranger may start a conversation on some current topic, and ask your opinion. The same friendliness is evident everywhere, from the four-year old who asks you the time to the friendly barman or waiter who becomes almost one of the family when you frequent a particular cafe or restaurant.

The Spanish have a naturally optimistic outlook on life, and try to enjoy it to the full. The foreigner is quickly accepted if he fits into their way of life and does not expect them to change to suit him.

Amando de Miguel has a theory that the outward cheerfulness of the Spaniard is designed to hide an internal melancholy and quotes a popular song: '*Cuando el español canta, no está contento, es que, cantando, ahoga su sufrimiento*'. (When the Spaniard sings, he is not content, he's drowning his sorrow by singing). Whatever the reason, the outward expression of the people of Spain is cheerfulness. While people of other races seem, at times, to be waiting for death as a happy release, the average Spaniard seems intent on getting the most out of life whether it be cutting meat in the market, serving in a bar, driving a taxi or running one of the largest national companies.

The tolerance of foreigners is another attractive Spanish trait. In the country, the sole English inhabitant in a hamlet may be called *el francés* (the Frenchman). To many older people all foreigners are Frenchmen and their habits are tolerated quite well.

Business life

To counter-balance the appeal of hospitality, team spirit and industry you will find the average Spaniard unwilling to write letters—everything is done by telephone or fax—and, worst of all, late.

The Spaniard may talk admiringly of British seriousness, for-mality and punctuality, but this is all theory. In Spain punctuality is almost a vice and if you arrive at the office at the right time for an appointment or earlier you may be made to feel very un-comfortable. You are expected to arrive about half an hour late, make a few comments on the terrible state of the traffic and the impossibility of parking, and then get down to work. This may be followed by a long but excellent lunch lasting from about 14.30 until 17.30 after which most people go home.

Regional characteristics

All generalisations are dangerous. Although Andalusians are popu-larly supposed to enjoy *fiestas*, song and dance, your neighbours from that region may be hardworking, clean and respectful, characteristics not attributed in general to people from the eight southernmost provinces.

However, allowing for those exceptions which prove the rule, you will find that the people in the north tend to be hearty eaters, good hosts, more industrious and better educated than their southern counterparts and more European in some respects. Of course, the northern peoples have their faults too. The people of Galicia, Cantabria, Asturias and the Basque Country have a liking for too much wine which results in unruly behaviour.

In Valencia and other eastern provinces where fruit has been grown for centuries, the people have a reputation for loving *fiestas*, being as tight with money as the Scots, and being as clean as the

French. Andalucía is the fun region, symbolised by the Costa del Sol, one of the wealthiest areas in Spanish territory—and where work never seems to be taken too seriously. A full description of each of the seventeen provinces may be found in *Time Off In Spain and Portugal* by Teresa Tinsley. *Berlitz Blueprint Spain* is another good guide.

8
Highlights of Spanish History

The 'United States of Spain'? This has been the objective of legislators ever since the death of General Franco in 1975 and for this reason: Spanish territory has been divided into seventeen regions, each having its own regional government, complete with a *Presidente* and variable number of ministers known as *consejeros* or regional variations of the title. The regional government has authority over public works, education, sanitary services and the like. The most powerful regional governments such as those of the Basque Region, Galicia and Cataluña even have their own police forces and tax collectors. They are generally more powerful than the other regions, reflecting the ancient kingdoms on which the regional divisions were made. Although there is a federal system it does not yet match that of the United States. However the idea exists and may well forge a link between modern Spain and its long and turbulent history.

A GLIMPSE OF PRE-ROMAN SPAIN

The Celts and the Iberos
The Iberos were the first to settle in the ancient Spain of classical times. They may have originated in the *Iberia Caucasica* (Africa). The principal tribes of the Iberos and their settlements were:

● The Cantabros in the area around Santander and Cantabria.

● The Carpetanos in the area around Toledo.

● The Ausetanos, Indigetes, Ilergetes, Ilergavones, and Layetanos north of the River Ebro.

● The Contestanos and Edetanos in Valencia.

- The Mastienos and Deitanos in Murcia.

- The Tartesios, Bastetanos and Oretanos in Andalucia.

- The Lusitanos in Portugal.

You will still come across some of these names, like *Cantabros*. The Via Leyetana is also a principal thoroughfare in Barcelona. Greek and Roman writers mention the Tartesios and their king Argantonio who reigned from 630 BC until 550 BC.

The Celts crossed the Pyrenees and invaded Spain in about 1200 BC, receiving further reinforcements in the sixth century BC. The Celts seem to have bypassed the Basque country. The Basque people seem to date from well before this period and the language defies all attempts to trace its origins. The principal tribes of the Celts and their associated regions were:

- The Artabros and the Calaeci in Galicia.

- The Berones in La Rioja.

- The Turmódigos in Burgos.

The two races of the Celts and the Iberos became well mixed throughout the remainder of the Iberian Peninsula. The result was the Celtiberic population and culture, an example of which is the *Dame de Elche*, the head of an ancient goddess found in south-east Spain in 1897. The principal Celt-iberic tribes and areas were:

- The Arevvacos in the upper part of the River Duero.

- The Belos in Medinaceli (famous for a unique Roman arch).

- The Lusones in Daroca and Calatayud (Zaragoza).

- The Pelendones in Soria.

- The Titos in Segorbe (Castellón).

The Celt-Iberos built fortified cities which were, in fact, city states. At times they united to fight common enemies. There is some evidence that all these tribes were governed by a senate of elders or princes and kings. The largest was the Tartesios.

Although the Celt-Iberos settled much of the Iberian Peninsula, others such as the Phoenicians colonised ports and other areas. King Argantonio of the Tartesios encouraged other peoples to establish colonies in Denia (Artemisión), Mainake (near Málaga), Corduba, Abdera and other locations.

All these states co-existed relatively peacefully.

However, when King Argantonio died, the Tartesios attacked the Phoenicians at Gadir (Cádiz) and began a round of wars which continued until the Roman occupation.

Carthage rules

The Phoenicians were quick to summon aid from their allies, the Carthaginians who established their first base in Ebusus (Ibiza) about 550 BC. The war went so well for the Carthaginians that they ended up ruling Cádiz and all the land around the southern and eastern coasts to the River Ebro. The Carthaginians eventually made a treaty with Rome that this would be the frontier. Later when Hannibal wished to make war on Rome he attacked the fortress city of Sagunto, some 30 kms to the north of Valencia.

THE ROMANS

Sagunto withstood a long siege, but eventually the inhabitants made the same decision as the Jews of Masada and chose to die rather than surrender. The siege ended in 218 BC but marked the beginning of the Second Punic War. Sagunto had signed a friendship treaty with the Romans and two hundred years of warfare began. The Roman war machine moved into top gear and utilised every means to conquer the Iberian Peninsula. The final battle of the war was waged against the last remaining Celt-Iberos, the Asturs and Cantabros. Caesar Augustus headed seven legions to defeat the remnants, successfully establishing the *pax romana* for nearly five hundred years. Four Roman emperors were born in Spain, Trajan, Adrian, Maximus and Theodosius. The provinces augmented in number from the original three, Bética, Tarraconse, and Lusitania to include Balearica, Gallaecia, Cartagunense and Tingutana.

At this point, between 19 BC and 15 BC, Zaragoza which had appeared in 550 BC as an Iberian walled city, was founded as a Roman city by Caesar Augustus and named Caesaraugusta after him. The veterans returned here from the Cantabrian war, the Fourth Legion (Macedon), the Fifth Legion (Alauda), the Sixth Legion (Victrix) and the Tenth Legion (Gémina).

The city of Caesaraugusta became an important Roman metropolis with four gates—Valencia, Toledo, Angel and Cineja. They were linked by the main streets of Cardo Maximus and Degvamnus Maximus. In 460 AD, the city was still flourishing under Roman rule when Emperor Majorianus visited it.

Just twelve years later it fell to an army of Goths commanded by Count Gauterico, and Roman supremacy was swept away by the armies of the Visigoths, Suevos and Franks.

CHRISTIANS AND MOSLEMS

By that time, Christianity was well established in Spain in spite of an inauspicious beginning. Christianity had been taken to Spain by road and ship and had met with severe persecution throughout Roman Spain (*Hispania*). The Pro-Consul, General Sergio Suplicius Galva published his imperial edict banning the faith and Gayo and Cremencia, the first martyrs, met their deaths in Zaragoza in 66 AD.

By the fourth century AD Zaragoza had become a base for evangelising, helped originally perhaps, by the apostle Paul who mentioned that he intended to visit Spain in Romans 15:24, 28. Whether he did or not you may see his statue at Tarragona celebrating his visit!

In 711 AD the Arabs invaded Spain under General Tariq ibn Ziyad who gave his name to Gibraltar (*Gibel—Tariq*, rock—Tariq). The general and his hosts used the Roman roads to sweep past the Visigoth resistance (which was greatly divided) and rapidly dominated the Iberian Peninsula. In the spring of 714 AD, Zaragoza was taken by Mussa, and its name changed to Sarakosta. Spain came under Arab domination and was declared an emirate. Arab domination in eighth century extended to France, Poitiers being the farthest point when the Arabs battled unsuccessfully with Charles Martel in 732 AD.

The far north of the Pyrenees was freed from Moorish occupation very quickly, by 737 AD, as was Asturias and Cantabria. This explains why the peoples of these regions have the most European appearance today. Exactly the opposite applies in the south of Spain where the Arab occupation lasted until the end of the fifteenth century. Visiting a bar in some parts of rural Andalucia may be similar to visiting a north African bar as far as the physiognomy of the occupants and occasionally, the character.

Zaragoza was returned to Christendom on 18th December 1118 AD when Alfonso I, *el Batallador*, conquered the city. He used his northern army of Bearnese, Borgonese, Aquitanos, Navarros and Aragonese to defeat the forces of Ali ben Yussuf, part of the process of overthrowing the Moors which lasted until 1492 AD when Granada was conquered.

The Arab occupation of Spain brought great benefits to Spain by introducing Arab art and craft and establishing important universities like the one in Cordoba, the southern capital.

The Reconquista (Re-conquest)

This word occurs millions of times in books devoted to Spanish history. It is used to describe the period of fighting between 722 AD after the Battle of Covadonga (721 AD) and 1492 when the Catholic Monarchs (los Reyes Católicos) took the last Moorish stronghold, Granada.

During the 781 years that the Arabs controlled the Iberian Peninsula, battles were waged back and forth, with alternate advances by Arab then Christian forces. Gradually the Christian kingdoms of the north emerged as Aragón, Asturias, Cantabria, Cataluña, León, Galicia, Navarra, Castilla (this is much of central Spain and takes its name from the great number of castles (*castillos*) built at that time). It is hard to calculate which areas belonged to which force at any period of time since some areas like León changed hands several times.

In the meantime in the south, rival factions divided the Arab world with the result that Spain was split into Arab kingdoms which grew smaller and smaller. This gave the Christians the opportunity to advance. If you are interested in Spanish history there are a great many books available on the subject and a surprisingly large number of original documents have survived. If you only have a passing interest, the outline of its history detailed here will help you appreciate the background of the many ancient and historic buildings that you will see.

On 2nd January 1492, King Fernando II of Aragón and Queen Isabel I of Castilla and León won the final victory over the Moorish forces at Granada. Spain had, at last, acquired national unity, which had been the monarchs' intention since their marriage in 1469 at Valladolid. They sent a letter on 2nd January to communicate the news to the *Consejo de Zaragoza*. It took thirteen days to arrive and the victory was celebrated with special processions on 15th, 16th and 17th January 1492. Pope Alexander VI gave the monarchs the title of *Los Reyes Católicos* as a reward for their achievement.

King Fernando II of Aragón proceeded to extend his dominions in many directions and his full title is Fernando V of Aragón, Castilla, Sicilia, and Napoles. He lived from 1452 until 1516 and was one of those rare individuals who seemed to know how to govern the unruly Spanish.

1492 was as fatal for the Jews in Spain and Portugal as it was for the Arabs. Many thousands of them were expelled and they fled to places as far apart as Wales, North Africa and Jerusalem. They speak a form of Spanish which dates from the fifteenth century and can be rather hard to understand. It is called Sephardim and you may still hear it in special programs on Hebrew radio stations. Some Sephardic families still possess the original key to the homestead they were forced to leave in 1492. Today, friendship programs exist in Spain and the *Sefardies* are frequent visitors, holding conferences in their former capitals such as Cordoba and Toledo.

CHRISTOPHER COLUMBUS AND LOS REYES CATOLICOS

1492, as has been mentioned elsewhere, is also the year the greatest land development voyage of all times concluded: Christopher Columbus made the first recorded landfall in the Americas on 12th October 1492. Altogether Columbus made four voyages across the Atlantic during the course of which he discovered San Salvador, Haiti, Cuba, other Caribbean islands and the coasts from the Orinoco to Caracas.

The complete records of his voyages have been preserved and make interesting reading. The first was written by Fray Bartolomé de las Casas. He records that Columbus would never tell his crew exactly how far they had travelled each day because he did not want the actual distance to frighten them. When Columbus landed on the island called *Guanahani* (the first day of the discovery of the New World), Fray Bartolomé noted the beauty of the nude natives greeting them and remarked that none seemed older than about thirty.

The record of the second voyage was written by Columbus and

given to don Antonio de Torres to give to *los Reyes Católicos*. He
also made the records of the third and fourth voyages. He liked to
be called *El Almirante* (the Admiral), a title which his descendants
still use.

Although *Los Reyes Católicos* backed Columbus at first, Court
intrigues later disgraced him. He died in near poverty, in Valladolid
on 20th May 1506 and left two wills which can be seen today. They
are dated 22nd February 1498 and 25th August 1505. The second
will bequeaths various sums of money to many people in Genoa:
Antonio Vazo, Luis Centurion Escoto, '*Jeronimo del Puerto, padre
de Benito del Puerto, Chanceller en Génova*' and *Paulo de Negro,
ginovés*.

If you mix with Spaniards at all you will soon hear a reference
to *huevo de Colon* (Columbus' egg). The story is told in all parts
of Spain and goes as follows:

'One day Columbus was with some of his enemies who tried to
make little of his great exploits. So Columbus asked them to
balance an egg on end on the table. All tried without success. Then
Columbus tapped one end of the egg and balanced it easily
(presumably it was hard-boiled like the ones you see in Spanish
bars today). They all replied that it was too easy and simple— but
Columbus replied with an ironic smile, "but it did not occur to
you first." '

MONARCHY AND REPUBLIC

The Habsburgs

Carlos I was the first Habsburg king and he came to the throne in
1516. He is remarkable for having founded the '*Archivo de
Escrituras Reales*' in 1509 to record deeds of castles, titles and all
royal business matters from mines to rents. This collection, now
known as the *Archivo de Simancas*, is kept in Valladolid and
numbers 33 million documents, or so it is claimed. The last
Habsburg king died in 1701 and Felipe V came to the throne.

The Bourbons

Carlos III was the most notable of the Bourbon kings. He reigned
from 1716 until 1768. He is considered to have been one of the
best Spanish kings. He established a Golden Age to the benefit of
the population. As you travel around Spain you will see many of
this king's architectural creations.

Fernando VII restored Bourbon rule in 1814 after the

Napoleonic occupation. As a result he was known as *El Deseado* (the Desired). However, he tore up the 1812 Constitution and became a tyrant. After that he was known as *El Rey Felón* (the King of Treachery). This restoration like some subsequent restorations of Bourbon rule was not a happy event.

The nineteenth century in Spain was characterised by the struggle between liberals and conservatives with varying degrees of success. Isabel II reigned from 1843 until 1868 when a republic was established by revolution.

In 1875 Bourbon rule was restored when General Martinez-Campos proclaimed Alfonso XII the next Bourbon monarch in January 1875. His reign was prosperous and peaceful for many Spaniards but it only lasted for ten years. He died of tuberculosis (as did his first wife) at the age of 28 in 1885. His second wife produced an heir posthumously, Alfonso XIII. There was a costly regency period during which Spain lost the last of its American possessions, Cuba, Puerto Rico and the Philippines.

MODERN POLITICAL LIFE

Alfonso XII ruled from 1906 until 1931 when he was forced to exile himself to Rome. The republic which succeeded him until 1936 (when the Civil War began) was violent in every way.

When the Civil War ended in 1939, liquidisations followed for the losers and years of starvation. The victors lived well under Generalismo Franco who lasted until 1975. In this year Bourbon rule was restored once more with King Juan Carlos and Queen doña Sofia, excellent monarchs, and very popular in Spain today.

The change to Bourbon rule after the dictatorship of Franco came more calmly than many observers believed possible and King Juan Carlos I immediately showed that he is a great believer in democracy. He receives all the party chiefs whether Communist or right wing.

In fact, the first elections brought a centre party to power which was headed by Adolf Suarez. He cleverly manoeuvred the country through the difficult times of great change. However, he decided to resign after a military take-over bid on 23rd February 1982. In the autumn elections, the Socialist Party, headed by Felipe Gonzalez, enjoyed a landslide victory.

Socialist domination, the current political situation
The period after 1982 was marked by a substantial majority with

La Línea dinástica española

1. **Vermudo I** de Cantabria, Rey de Asturias en 788 AD padre de
2. **Ramiro I**, Rey de Asturias, padre de
3. **Ordoño I**, Rey de Asturias, padre de
4. **Alfonso III**, Rey de Asturias, padre de
5. **Ordoño II** Rey de León, padre de
6. **Ramiro II**, Rey de León, padre de
7. **Ordoño III**, Rey de León, padre de
8. **Vermudo II**, Rey de León, padre de
9. **Alfonso V**, Rey de León, padre de
10. **Sancha** Reina de León, casada con Fernando I de Castilla, padres de
11. **Alfonso VI**, Rey de Castilla y de León, padre de
12. **Urraca I**, Reina de Castilla y de León, casada con Raimundo de Borgoña, padres de
13. **Alfonso VII**, Emperador y Rey de Castilla y de León, padre de
14. **Fernando II**, Rey de León, padre de
15. **Alfonso IX**, Rey de León, padre de
16. **Fernando III**, Rey de Castilla y de León, padre de
17. **Alfonso X**, Rey de Castilla y de León, padre de
18. **Sancho IV**, Rey de Castilla y de Leó, padre de
19. **Fernando IV**, Rey de Castilla y de León, padre de
20. **Alfonso XI**, Rey de Castilla y de León, padre de
21. **Enrique II**, Rey de Castilla y de León, padre de
22. **Juan I**, Rey de Castilla y de León, padre de
23. **Enrique III** Rey de Castilla y de León, padre de
24. **Juan II**, Rey de Castilla y de León, padre de
25. **Isabel I**, Reina de Castilla y de León, casada con Fernando II de Aragón, padres de
26. **Juana I** de España casada con Felipe de Austria, padres de
27. **Carlos I**, padre de
28. **Felipe II**, padre de
29. **Felipe III**, padre de
30. **Felipe IV**, padre de
31. **Maria Teresa**, Infanta de España, casada con Luis XIV de Francia, padres de
32. **Luis (de Borbón)**, Delfin de Francia, padre de
33. **Felipe V**, padre de
34. **Carlos III**, padre de
35. **Carlos IV**, padre de
36. **Fernando VII**, padre de
37. **Isabel II**, casada con el Infante Don Francisco de Asis de Borbón, padres de
38. **Alfonso XII**, padre de
39. **Alfonso XIII**, padre de
40. **Juan**, Conde de Barcelona, padre de
41. **Juan Carlos I.**

Fig. 16. Genealogy of the Spanish royal family. Established for twelve centuries it is the oldest-reigning monarchy in Europe. Reproduced by permission of *Diario ABC de Madrid*. *Padre de* = father of. *Padres de* = parents of. *Casada con* = married to. *Rey/Reina* = King/Queen. *Conde de* = Count of.

a 'steam-roller' vote which ensured that the government's wishes were obeyed and rubber-stamped by the Cortes, (Parliament). The Socialist Party had maintained an internal discipline, permitting nobody to resign thus making for a stable government. Scandal after scandal was unearthed but public enquiries were never permitted and ministers remained at their posts.

During the 1980s many allegations were made against the brother of the Vice President of the Government. Juan Guerra was accused of using his influence and of being involved in numerous scandals. Each time Alfonso Guerra tendered his resignation and each time the President, Felipe Gonzalez, refused to accept it.

In 1991, the formal legal proceedings against Juan Guerra began to show that there was truth in the allegations and that he had amassed a considerable private fortune during the period that the Socialists had been in power. Alfonso Guerra immediately offered to resign again. This time his resignation was accepted and the powerful coalition broken between the President who governs and the Vice President who continues to control the Socialist Party.

It is a puzzle to decide which faction of the Party is favoured by Felipe Gonzalez who was well trained by the Swedish Premier Olaf Palmer, now dead. Almost all of the important posts have been infiltrated by the Socialists from football clubs to the highest spheres. The Opposition remains as weak as ever, currently headed by a youthful leader. Even if the Opposition were strong it would find it difficult to change the political tide. However, it has to be said that the Minister of Economy, Carlos Solchaga, who leads the right wing, is gaining power.

On the one hand the Government has the support of those who hold sinecures, who are in work but claim unemployment benefit and others benefiting from corrupt practices. On the other hand, Spanish Socialism is right wing, nearer the social democrats, which antagonises the unions and at the same time support in the larger cities seems to be waning judging from the results of the last municipal elections. The Socialists even lost Seville, the home land of Felipe Gonzalez and the Guerra family. However Felipe Gonzalez is confident enough to have offered his services as President of a coalition government, and he certainly seems able 'to rule the roost' in Spain, always a difficult task given the unruly national character.

9
Holidaying in Spain

The scenery in the Iberian Peninsula is as varied as the types of transport available. If you are not in a hurry you could take a donkey taxi in Mijas, Costa del Sol. There is a boom in regional airlines and jetfoils cut journey times between the Canary Islands, crossing the Straits of Gibraltar and in the Balearic Islands.

Trains may prove their utility by luxury trips to help you become better acquainted with Spain, links overnight with Paris or (down the price scale) day trips. AVE means bird in Spanish but this 'bird' will never fly as it is the acronym for the new Spanish high speed train, ready to start in 1992, this special year for Spain. It is planned that the AVE will link Barcelona (the Olympic city) with Seville (the World Exhibition). The train will shuttle between these two cities via Madrid at 300 kmph. Also, new railway routes are planned to speed travel with modern trains which will link into the European network.

AIR TRAVEL

Aviaco has been the Spanish domestic airline for a long time. It uses DC-9 and F-27 aeroplanes providing links between the smaller cities such as Vigo, Zaragoza, La Coruña and the main industrial centres. Some complain that there are too many airports in Spain so do not be surprised to find one not too far away from what you thought was quite an out of the way place.

The choice of airline is getting wider every day with 1992, and then 1993 with its promise of free markets. As so many small airports and regional services are becoming available it is a good idea to make your travel agent check properly. His list may not be up to date. Here are some of the most recently announced airlines.

- LAE (*Lineas Aereas Extremenas*). F-27s are used to link

Madrid and Badajoz twice daily. There are plans to link in Barcelona, Bilbao, Valencia and other cities.

- Binter Canarias is a subsidiary of IBERIA and offers rapid connections to the Canary Islands using CN-235s, ATR-72s and DC-9s.

- Binter Mediterranea SA will link the Spanish mainland to the Balearic Islands and in the future North Africa, southern France and Italy.

- Binter Centro is to provide air links between Madrid and cities in the interior of Spain.

- Norjet flies from the airports of Vitoria and Bilbao to Europe and the rest of Spain. It is the first Basque airline.

- LAC (Lineas Aereas Canarias) uses MD-83s to ferry passengers from and around the Canary Islands to northern Europe.

- Air Sur began life in 1990 and was the first private line to be allowed to operate scheduled passenger services between Madrid and Valladolid. The service has since been extended to include Barcelona, Málaga and Seville.

- Baron von Wernitz plans complete coverage of the north coastal zone with his private airline, Wernitz Air. The company was formed in 1989 but ran into trouble. It should be functioning now.

- Binter Norte will cover the north coastal zone too when the authorisation has been processed.

It is likely that this list will grow since there are many other projects in hand and tourism is flourishing.

TRAVELLING BY SEA

There are many useful ferries serving the islands and Africa. Jetfoil services are proving very popular with those who like to cut travelling time to a minimum and enjoy the sensation of travelling over the waves. And for those who like the idea of something exotic a transparent submarine is on order from Finland for use in the Balearics.

Jetfoil services

The papers greeted the advent of the first jetfoil in Spain with headlines such as 'The First European', 'Best In The World' and so on despite the fact that the jetfoil has been well known for decades. The services link Spanish ports, the Canary Islands and cross the Straits of Gibraltar from Algeciras to Ceuta. It is planned to serve Melilla too. These services are organised by *Compañia Trásmediterranea*.

Private services are also being developed. There is a summer only service from Denia on the Costa Blanca to Alicante and Ibiza. Other routes are under consideration. This also applies to Gibraltar. A jetfoil service could alleviate conditions in holiday periods. Immigrant Arab workers wishing to return home at these times create chaos. The Red Cross provides special temporary shelters for them. If you are planning to use this ferry crossing it is best to avoid July and August as an extremely long wait in trying circumstances is likely.

Sea ferries

The *Compañia (Cia) Trásmediterranea* has a long history of providing strategic connections between the Spanish mainland and the many islands under the Spanish flag. The fleet consists of about forty vessels which provide overnight services from Valencia to Majorca, Menorca, Ibiza and connections to Formentera. The same applies from Barcelona and the Balearic Islands, Cádiz and the Canary Islands, Algeciras and North Africa. In slack periods the ferries are used for cruises. If you have the time, a voyage can be more enjoyable than a flight and you can take your car too.

Owing to EEC regulations and pressure from other companies, *Trásmediterranea* no longer has the monopoly on these services. Isnasa (*Isleña de Navigación*) is one rival. It operates four ferries providing eight services daily on the Algeciras-Ceuta route, six to Tangier and one from La Tarifa to Tangier.

Smaller companies ply between some ports but *Trásmediterranea* and Isnasa are the two main companies.

OVERLAND ON THE TRAIN

Special day excursion trains

The State railway company, RENFE (*Red Nacional de Ferro-carriles Españoles*), introduced these in recent years in Madrid. They offer day trips to historical sites and the price includes the train fare, guides, and entrance fees to the places visited.

The star attraction is the excursion train to Aranjuez which was mentioned in Chapter 1. The line to Aranjuez was opened in 1850. The train you will take is steam-hauled using the original wooden rolling-stock. Hostesses in nineteenth century costume will offer you strawberries and when you arrive the town band will serenade you.

Similar trains run to Avila, the most impressive walled city in Spain, and Siguenza which has a cathedral, restored castle and historical buildings. These trains use more modern rolling-stock but passengers still receive special treatment. Day trips to be recommended also are those to El Escorial and Toledo amongst others.

Day trips organised by RENFE currently cost 1,500 pesetas. Some of the excursions from Madrid are:

● *Ciudad de Toledo* (City of Toledo).

● *Murallas de Avila* (Walls of Avila).

● *Doncel de Siguenza* (Master of Siguenza).

● *Monasterio de Piedra* (Monastery of Rock).

● *Ciudad Encantado de Cuenca* (Enchanted city of Cuenca).

Day trips from Barcelona are:

● *Delta del Ebro*.

● *Torre Galatea*.

● *Rutas del Cister*.

From Seville: *Tierras de Jerez* (Lands of Jerez).

Fig. 17. The Spanish railway system.

From Valencia: *Papa Luna* (the Pope Luna—Peñíscola).

Special weekend excursions
RENFE also organises a number of weekend excursions, leaving
on Friday evening and returning Monday morning. The prices
vary according to which trip you decide to take but they start
currently at 6,750 pesetas per person. All excursions start from
Madrid at the moment but RENFE is planning to introduce others
in different regions to help you become better acquainted with
Spain. Some of the lesser known sites and cities have been chosen
for these trips. They are all worth a weekend visit and will give
you an insight into the interior of Spain, enabling you to appreciate
the wealth of religious and historical buildings. Some trips,
however, should be avoided in the height of summer. The price
does include rail travel, accommodation, guided visits. Excursions
currently on offer are:

- *Ciudad Monumental de Cáceres* (Monumental city of Cáceres).

- *Románico de Zamora* (Romanesque of Zamora).

- *Camino de Soria* (Road to Soria).

- *Palencia: Camino de Santiago y Románico del Norte* (Palencia:
  Road to Santiago and Romanesque of the North).

- *Tierras del Cid* (Lands of the Cid).

Private enterprise is also entering this field. There is already one
such train operating from Benidorm to Denia and others are
planned.

Luxury trains
There are two extra special trains well worth the effort and expense.
These are *El Andalus* and *El Transcantábrico*. They rival the Orient
Express in the de luxe furnishings and fittings throughout.
  El Andalus travels from Seville via Córdoba and Granada to
Málaga and back again. If the entire trip is too expensive for you
or you cannot spare so much time, it is possible to travel from
Seville to Córdoba or Málaga to Seville. Great sensitivity to
passenger comfort has been shown since the train makes an
overnight stop in a siding to allow passengers to sleep instead of

subjecting them to the discomforts of the Andalucian track. The route has also been specially designed to avoid as much as possible exposing passengers to the excessive heat of the Andalucian summer. The sleeping cars and suites were built in France in 1929 for the King of England to exacting standards, using expensive woods to create luxury decor. You too may enjoy living like royalty.

At the moment the whole journey, if taken in May or June, costs 95,000 pesetas per person in a double sleeper, including meals in the restaurant. The price rises to 130,000 pesetas if you prefer a suite. The cheapest fare is from Málaga to Seville early in the year, 30,000 pesetas. The highest you may expect to pay, in September and October, is 115,000 pesetas or 150,000 pesetas for a suite.

On other occasions *El Andalus* heads north from Barcelona to Santiago de Compostela, returning via Pamplona, Burgos, León, Logroño and Zaragoza. On the return journey you may leave the train at Zaragoza or board it. This train allows you to visit many of the best tourist areas in complete luxury. The summer trip currently costs 99,000 pesetas per person in a double sleeper, 140,000 pesetas for a suite.

The same applies to another northern tourist train, *El Trans-cantábrico*. It costs about the same price, but this time you spend a week visiting the north and west, starting from León and visiting Bilbao, Santander, various other northern towns and terminating in El Ferrol. Attractions include stops in out of the way villages to see folk customs and enjoy typical picnic meals. Included in the price are some meals in the luxury Paradors and other extras.

Normal train services

There is a large variety of train services in Spain, ranging from the overnight luxury expresses to the railways of FEVE in the northern coastal region where wooden seats may still be found. Many improvements are being introduced. The Common Market is making grants available on a massive scale and the State is underwriting losses so that new rolling-stock may be introduced.

There is a train from Madrid to Moscow. It takes about three days with several changes of wheel gauge and has been very popular since the thaw in the East.

There are suburban services from all the large cities, but you must not expect them to resemble services in the United Kingdom. A 30 kms journey from Madrid can and does take an hour or more if the crews decide to strike. Striking is possible in the first six months of the year when the unions are negotiating the annual contract. Promises are continually being made to improve the *cercanias* (suburban services) and double level passenger carriages are being introduced. Any real improvement, however, in customer services, reducing the time it takes to make short journeys and so on still seem to be light years away.

For this reason business men rarely commute to work. The car is preferred as a means of transport which helps to explain the massive traffic jams at peak times in Spanish towns and cities. Some businessmen like to use the night trains which connect all the main cities and run to time.

Most Spanish cities are linked by a variety of trains. You may take an intercity train to Valencia from Madrid or Barcelona to Zaragoza, travelling in air conditioned bliss. Services include waiters with trays of airline meals, buffet car open for the entire journey and entertainment such as television and video films. Again times could be improved and there are frequent delays. Intercity trains generally have first class and second class accommodation.

Prices vary widely but if you are a traveller on a low budget *literas* could be the answer. You pay for a bed in a compartment containing six berths. It is customary to sleep fully dressed as you cannot be sure whether you will be sharing the compartment with a beautiful American girl or an immigrant Arab worker. Conversation may be polyglot in character and may continue into the small hours. The prospect of a good night's sleep is small under these circumstances when you consider that someone is bound to snore.

The worst experience you will encounter is travelling on the Lusitania Express, overnight from Madrid to Lisbon. It is definitely an experience for the young at heart, not for those who value their creature comforts. The train reaches the Border in the very small hours of the morning when even the most inveterate talker has fallen asleep. The Portuguese frontier police and Customs officers proceed to invade the train and take over. They insist on seeing passports, ID cards and other documentation while the Customs officer interrogates you. The main aim seems to be to discourage you from visiting their country.

Of course you may opt for something more comfortable. First class travel in a seat is preferred by many and the seats are quite wide. The Wagons-lits are usually good, if you are affluent. Night travel in Andalucia is not to be recommended.

By contrast, the overnight train from Madrid to Paris is excellent. There is a wide range of services available from normal to luxury sleepers, restaurant car, showers, air conditioning.

The following accommodation is available on night trains. You pay your money and take your choice.

● Third class seat.

● *Literas*, (sleeper bunk, six to a compartment).

● First class seat in an express.

● Normal sleeper.

● Luxury sleeper accommodation available on the Madrid— Paris route and a few others.

Locomotives available

The introduction of the AVE will enhance rail travel in Spain. It is an extension of the TGV, high velocity units which operate in France and Germany and will use the same gauge as the rest of Europe. At the moment all trains stop at the frontier to adapt to the different gauge. The exact entry points into Spain are still a matter of heated discussion as both the Basques and Catalans wish to claim the privilege of the European linkage. In spite of this the route from Seville to Madrid has been agreed and the track is now under construction. It follows an entirely new route incorporating many tunnels. After Madrid only time will tell which towns the railway will pass through on its way to Europe. At least you should be able to enjoy rapid train travel to Seville. At the moment some expresses may take 20 hours to travel from Barcelona to Seville.

Apart from this, the principal types of train that you will meet are the following.

● *Talgo*. This is a Spanish train on a triangular suspension provided by two wheels and a cantilever beam to the next coach. It is fast and usually quite comfortable.

● *Ter*. This is a well built Italian train from FIAT. It is high off the ground, comfortable and has a suspension which allows you to write when travelling at high speed.

● *Electro-Tren*. This is a modern Spanish built unit with video and cafeteria services. It is used on medium length journeys.

● *Regional Express*. This consists of modern suburban coaches

which should provide air conditioning and few other amenities.
They link Madrid with smaller provincial capitals.

- *Interurbano*. This is the Spanish equivalent of the suburban
  line. It has modern carriages, often crowded, and it usually
  runs late. It may be affected by strikes and is not advised for
  business commuters.

Ski Trains

These are a novelty recently introduced by RENFE and there are
two trips on offer. Remember to check the snow conditions with
the Spanish ski and mountain association before you book either
of these. Tel: (974) 22 56 56.

The first is in the *Sierra Nevada*. The trip includes the return
rail journey from Madrid to Granada, and accommodation in the
Sierra Nevada, 30 kms from Granada. The ski slopes are between
the altitudes of 2,100 and 3,470 metres above sea level and snow
coverage continues late into the year. There are some twenty ski
lifts for which you may obtain a season ticket. There are also
instructors and classes and you are allowed the run of the resort
with all its many amenities.

The other ski train is called the *Tren Blanco Estrella Pirineo*. It
travels overnight from Madrid either to Jaca for the ski resorts of
Candanchú and Astun or to Canfranca for the ski resorts of
Formigal and Panticosa. There is a wide variety of train and hotel
accommodation available. Jaca is a delightful little town which has
an ice rink, ancient part and shops to supply all your needs. The
hotels provide such large meals that it is advisable to eat only two
meals a day. The same applies to resorts in Andorra.

The pros and cons of train travel

These are the advantages of train travel in Spain:

- You can visit interesting places relatively cheaply.

- You may obtain deep insights into the wealth of history
  exemplified by the physical survival of so many ancient
  buildings, documents and relics.

- The timetable is restful.

- The routes are specially planned to avoid the worst of the summer heat.

These are the disadvantages:

- Train travel may be very slow.

- The guides usually speak in Spanish—except on the most expensive excursions.

- Day trippers to Aranjuez must endure the wooden seats in the period rolling-stock.

- Toilets on many trains in Spain leave much to be desired.

ACCOMMODATION

Paradores Nacionales

These State hotels are highly recommended for leisurely stays. Many are conversions of ancient historic buildings such as castles, palaces and monasteries. They offer modern comfort while preserving the atmosphere of the past. They are normally to four or five star standard and offer reasonable service with good cuisine. They will open your eyes to the wealth and might of Spain as a superpower of yesteryear. These buildings were built from the proceeds of some of the Spanish treasure galleons which arrived safely.

The Central Booking Office in Madrid (open from 09.30 until 13.30 and 16.30 until 19.30) can provide a booklet which lists almost all of the hotels in the chain with photographs. It is better to use the latest booklet as the less profitable hotels are sold or closed. Tel: (91) 435 97 00.

It would be a millionaire's dream to stay in each and every one of these Paradors, from Monte Perdido in the Pyrenees in a beautiful snowy valley to the most western and southern on the island of La Gomera in the Canaries. You can decide whether to sleep in the same room as King Carlos V in the castle of Jarandilla de la Vera or dine in the students' hospice in the university of Alcalá de Henares.

Advantages of staying in a PN:
- You can book them in advance from any part of the world.

- There is a high standard of service and cleanliness.

- The cuisine is excellent, normally to international standards and caters for all tastes.

- The buildings are usually interesting but the facilities are modern.

- They are frequently located in beauty spots which are off the beaten track for tourists.

- There are polyglot receptionists who are anxious to make your stay pleasant.

- Many provide a restful environment and have a bird's eye view of the local surroundings.

Disadvantages of staying in a PN:
- They are expensive.

- At peak times of the year, bookings may be limited to three or four days.

- You usually need to book well in advance.

- Some of the modern PNs are right next to old cities and one feels that one of the old buildings should have been made available for conversion.

If you do not wish to stay in one of these Paradors or cannot afford it, you will find them open for refreshments from 8.00 until 22.00. The buffet breakfast is worth mentioning. You may choose from a selection of bacon, eggs, sausages, ham (York), a wide range of cold meats, cheeses, patés and Spanish ham (*serrano*). This is followed by all kinds of cake, fruits and fruit juices. You may go up as many times as you like. If the waitress seems a little worried she may want to know your room number (¿'*Su numero de habitación, por favor?*'). If you have only called in for breakfast you should reply, '*estamos de paso*,' and ask for the bill when you have finished.

Spas
There are numerous spas scattered around the Iberian Peninsula.

These will take you back to the last century with its leisurely way of life and treatments which range from a rest cure to a full medical program controlled by doctors and staff. You may obtain information about these by writing to the address given in Chapter 5. Tel: (91) 542 97 75.

There are several good spas in Aragón (the northern provinces of Zaragoza and Huesca) including the spectacular spa in the valley of the Panticosa, 1,600 metres above sea level. There are several three star hotels and good skiing. The spa is located 54 kms from Jaca and 97 kms from Huesca in the southern Pyrenees and is recommended.

Fourteen of Spain's seventeen regions have these spas which are still popular. It is a good idea to check them carefully before you go to stay there as they can be very expensive.

Hotel chains
Tourism is a vital industry to Spain and has resulted in thousands of hotels of all kinds. It can be difficult to find a suitable hotel when travelling and if you cannot afford to stay in PNs it may be wisest to choose a hotel in a chain. Here are some examples.

Cadena Husa
The *Grupo Husa* was founded in 1930 and has become well established in Spain. Many of their hotels are to be found on the Mediterranean seaboard but there are some in other parts of Spain and in Kuwait, Puerto Rico, Budapest and Miami. The head office is in Barcelona. It is a card company. Tel: (91) 276 71 86).

Grupo Sol
This concern has a great many hotels in the Balearics and most beachside areas. It caters mostly for the package tour trade so millions recall stays in their hotels. Although most of the hotels are in the resorts, this chain is expanding to other areas of Spain and other countries. There is good service and good food. The Sol group offer a 'Prestige' card entitling you to preferential treatment and sometimes a discount. It can be useful if you make frequent trips and it can be used in Melia hotels too. You may obtain the card from head office in Palma de Mallorca. Tel: (871) 29 89 66.

Melia Hotels
This chain chiefly provides five star hotels in the main cities. The motto of this chain is 'every room in the hotel is the best'. The

cuisine is good and breakfast substantial. These hotels are ideal for long business lunches. Tel: (91) 241 82 00.

Novotel

This company is opening new hotels in Spain such as the Novotel Madrid which is close to the motorway leading to the airport. There are ample conference rooms and facilities for business meetings. Tel: (91) 405 46 00.

TRYP Hotels

This chain is a relative newcomer to Spain using foreign capital. There is now a whole chain of four.or five star hotels throughout the country. Tel: (91) 315 32 46.

HOTUSA Hotels

These are increasingly seen in Spain and Spain now accounts for about half of the hotels this company holds. Tel: (93) 318 45 75.

Santos Hotels

This is a small company with two hotels in Madrid and one in Santander. The hotels are specially designed for business meetings, meals, cocktails. Tel: (91) 431 21 37.

Familia Hotels

This is an organisation of some seventy family hotels. It specialises in providing accommodation at reasonable prices for large families. The *familia numerosa* is still quite common in Spain and is a steady market force. Hotels are usually one to three star grade, each being run by a family with the idea of making other families feel at home. Its policy statement reads, 'a small hotel with a straightforward, friendly, family atmosphere and good sensible cooking'. This organisation is associated with 550 hotels throughout Europe including Consort Hotels in the United Kingdom, Neotel in France, HTR hotels in Austria, Landidyll in Germany, CMV Hotels in Ireland.

Familia Hotels pay great attention to good service in many ways. It provides a tourist map of Spain marking the hotels in the organisation and a booklet with the details of each hotel in the chain in six languages: English, French, German, Italian, Spanish and Catalan. The hotel Conde de Aznar in Jaca in the southern Pyrenees is recommended. Tel: (93) 317 92 16.

Possible perks

If you plan to travel a great deal in Spain for business, pleasure or other reasons, it is useful to know that some of the hotel chains give cards to clients which may reduce the price of a room by 10 per cent, or in special cases, 25 per cent.

Private hotels

The advantage of staying in hotels belonging to a recognised chain is that if you have a complaint, it is more likely to be taken seriously. Foreign visitors are commenting increasingly on the worsening service in many Spanish hotels. Requesting the complaint book or form (*libro de reclamaciones o hoja*) usually has some effect. The quality of Spanish private hotels is very variable. Using one in a chain of hotels usually guarantees a degree of satisfaction.

There are good individual hotels to be found. They certainly exist but it may involve a number of unpleasant experiences before you find one. The Hotel Puerto de Pajares on the road from Asturias to Madrid is greatly recommended. It used to be a PN but is now run by the regional government at reasonable prices. It is especially attractive to groups interested in winter sports or hill walking, mountaineering and the like. Tel: (985) 49 60 23.

LEISURE ACTIVITIES

Twenty or thirty years ago it used to be necessary to explain to the majority of Spaniards (not the travelled upper class) what 'tennis' and 'golf' were. Since then there have been many successful Spanish champions in these sports and in others less well known. Spain has become a country for tennis, golf, camping, yachting, skiing, caving and many other pastimes.

The younger generation are taking a greater interest in sports these days and facilities which were scarce two decades ago are now common. Of course, all the Olympic sports have been given a tremendous boost since the Olympic Games are to be held in Barcelona in 1992. In addition, the southern Pyrenean town of Jaca is bidding for the 1996 Winter Olympics so attention is being focused on those activities too. *Mercanza* (sponsorship, patronage) is becoming widespread in Spain. Companies are not only sponsoring the Spanish Olympic teams in all kinds of sport from sailing to fencing but also cultural events.

Lovers of classical music, theatre, films and the other arts are

well catered for. Any of the multitude of tourist offices will give
you information on the subject. Granada has a very good classical
music festival. Film festivals are staged every year at San Sebastián,
Alcalá de Henares, Valladolid and other capitals. They are becoming sufficiently important to attract top stars.

You will find many suggestions in the national Press and the
many foreign language publications in Spain can be very helpful.
They list not only golf clubs, football and activities of general
interest to Spaniards but also such activities as amateur theatricals,
organised walks, art classes, cricket, bowls, Samaritans Worldwide,
cottage artistry, barbecuing, polo, bridge, harriers, mountain walking, American football, animal protection societies, cross country
running and so on. You might even find a train spotting club if
you try hard enough!

In Spain leisure activities have given rise to important industries
as much as anywhere else. Special areas of growth are golf, marinas
and athletics (because of the Olympics). Even the smallest town is
installing a swimming pool in the hope of encouraging a gold
medallist.

Benalmádena is a perfect example of the kind of development
that is taking place. Senor don Ramón Rico-Muñoz has been the
mayor of Benalmádena since 1st December 1985 and one of his
principal aims is to put Benalmádena on the map. It is the first
resort on the Costa del Sol to have drawn up its own marketing
plan. Senor Rico states to all and sundry, 'We are the first town
too of our size to offer so many cultural events which include
classical concerts, folk dancing and so on. We aim to promote our
offer year round'. International football teams make use of this
town's facilities for training as well as the locals.

Golf

The golf enthusiast will find his paradise on the Costa del Sol
where there are a score of first class golf courses within a few miles
of each other, many with built in luxury housing developments.
New golf courses are being projected, planned and built all the
time so the selection is very wide. You should contact the
Andalucian Golf Federation if you would like the latest, most
detailed information. Tel: (952) 22 59 90.

Some of the latest news is that a Swedish company has bought
Los Naranjos Golf Club and is improving the quality of the Robert
Trent Jones course and building a new clubhouse. The Swedish
Conata group has put up 50 per cent of the capital for the Waconsa

group to build a new leisure facility comprising luxury housing and a golf course designed by Severiano Ballesteros and José Luis de Bernardo. It is called *Los Arqueros*, is due to be completed by July 1991 and is 10 kms from Marbella. It is thought that it will become part of the Royal Spanish Golf Federation and that it may be the venue for important tournaments.

A new course called Domayo in Galicia is being opened. It is 8 kms from Vigo and 10 kms from Pontevedra and lies beside the River Vigo, commanding exceptional views.

Veragolf is another new course designed by Seve Ballesteros. It is on the coast of Almeria and its opening is planned to coincide with the 500th anniversary of Columbus' arrival in the Americas, in 1992. Again it will be a golf course and luxury housing development.

There are currently seven courses in Majorca and one each on Ibiza and Menorca, but four more are being built: Roca Viva, 71 kms from Palma de Mallorca at Capdepera, Son Termens, 12 kms from Palma de Mallorca on the Carretera de Bunyola, Santa Pinca, 18 kms from Palma de Mallorca on the Carretera de Andraix, Ibiza's new golf course, 8 kms from Elvissa on the Carretera de Sta Eulalia por Jesús.

The Balearic Golf Federation is helpful and will send information to foreign visitors and the Govern Balear will also have all the information about golf courses in the region. The Spanish themselves treat golf as something of a status symbol, making great play of using the English words, just like bottles of Scotch whisky and the pedigree dog with its British name. As Amando de Migueles writes in *Los Españoles*, 'Leisure time has less to do with Nature than might be expected. It is true that everyone says that they like the countryside, the beach, the mountains; but the favourite pastimes of the Spanish are watching television, listening to the radio and using the car'.

In spite of this definition which is mainly true, golf is a booming sport together with yachting and all concerning leisure boating.

Marinas and 'mucking about in boats'

Spain is the country with the greatest number of public holidays per year in the Common Market, and these holidays alone give Spaniards plenty of time for nautical sports. Then there are normal holidays, adding an extra month or so. It is hardly surprising that marinas are mushrooming around the Spanish mainland and archipelagos. All the associated nautical sports are enjoying similar popularity. In fact, such is the popularity that even the inland province of Guadalajara has sponsored a Soling class sailing boat for the 1992 Olympics and has declared itself an open port using the inland lake of Entrepeñas for the Master 470 Cup.

The market for new boats in Spain is said to be the most flourishing in the Mediterranean. On the Costa del Sol, in 1989, experts say that there were boat sales of over 8 billion pesetas. You will find a great selection of services offered, berthing and storage facilities. The Spanish Customs permits foreign registered boats to be used for six months of the year and to remain in the country for the rest of the year during which time the boat may be used for habitation. Gibraltar has two marinas which bring in 5 million per year in boat business and upkeep.

A new luxury marina and tourist development is to be built on the coast of Almeria province called Puerto Marques. It will comprise marinas, two golf courses, hotels, commercial centres and much housing. There is an international airport near Almeria now and roads are being upgraded so this area will finally be developed.

The number of marinas continues to increase in the Canary Islands too. There are now four on Tenerife, four in Gran Canaria and one each on the isles of Gomera, La Palma, Lanzarote and Fuerteventura. They are all close to airports and popular because of the year long season. Many people keep their craft on these islands since it is only 705 nautical miles from Cádiz to Tenerife and 680 nautical miles from Cádiz to Gran Canaria.

Tennis
Tennis is practised everywhere these days, helped greatly by some of the Spanish stars. Several of these, incidentally, are emigrating to Andorra to enjoy their earnings without having to pay tax. Every small town, hotel and club has its tennis court so this game may be practised year round in many parts of Spain. There are even flood-lit courts like those at the Motel Avión near Madrid's Barajas airport. Manuel Santana also owns and runs one of the best European tennis schools in Puente Romana (Málaga).

Other sports
It would require a book in itself to detail the many sports on offer in Spain. The Spanish Sports Council (*Consejo Superior de Deportes*) will supply a great deal of information about sports and

the many federations which cover every activity from caving to clay pigeon shooting and rally driving. The address is: Avda Martin Fierro s/n, 28003 Madrid. Tel: (91) 449 73 00.

High quality hunting, shooting and fishing are available in Spain from salmon fishing in the northern rivers to shooting mountain goats in the Sierra de Gredos. But you must make sure that you have the right permit and know which species are protected. Shooting a bear for example carries a £5,000 penalty and a jail sentence. Small game and fishing licences are easy to obtain.

For those with a love of the wild open spaces, all is possible in Spain with the many sierras and mountain ranges. Hiking is not popular among the Spanish. You may see a great many youths with impressive camping kit at the railway stations in the Sierras at weekends. They will be making a beeline for the nearest campsite to spend the weekend with the girlfriend. As the Spanish seem to have a limited knowledge of Nature you will probably find field mushrooms in abundance at the right season.

The mountains
Some of the mountain areas in Spain are well worth exploring on your travels around Spain like the mountains of Asturias, and moving eastwards, the Picos de Europa. The Pyrenees are a world in themselves and are now being developed as a separate region on both sides of the frontier. Jaca, St Jean Pied de Port, the Valle de Aran and Andorra are all to be recommended.

The central zones of Spain have sierras too. Gredos often has snowfalls and is surprisingly isolated, as is the Sierra de Malagón. The Sierra de Navacerrada is very popular with the Madrileños and parking can be a problem. The Sierra Nevada near Granada is also well developed.

Northern Spain
The north and north west coastal regions are also not as well known to many foreigners. There is excellent scenery, very long attractive beaches and it has long been the haunt of the wealthy Spaniard during his holidays. This included Franco. It is also ideal for those who prefer a cooler climate and rural surrounds. Galicia with its Rías Bajas and Rías Altas is an old favourite with the Spanish and well worth getting to know.

Where to eat

Eating places are best judged by the size of the clientèle. Expensive restaurants with few diners should be avoided and you should patronise those that are well frequented. The Spanish enjoy eating out so the best places will be obvious by the crowds.

HASTA LA VISTA

So we come to the end of this book, and hope that like a good meal it will leave a good taste in your mouth for living and working in Spain. Of the millions who flock to Spain each year, increasing numbers have converted their holiday homes into permanent residences. Perhaps you will be among them? Whether you plan to stay for a short while or for rather longer, we'll say 'Hasta la vista!'

Useful Contacts

EMBASSIES AND CONSULATES

The British Consulate, Edificio Cataluña PO Box 2020, 5 Luis Morote 6-3, Puerto de la Luz, 35007 Las Palmas, Canary Islands. Tel: 26 25 08. Telex: 95276 a/b 95276 BRLTP E, fax: 267774.

The British Consulate, Plaza Nueva 8-Dpdo, 41001 Seville. Tel: 422 88 75. Telex: 72107 a/b BPSE V E, fax: 22 88 74.

The British Consulate-General, Avda de la Fuerzas, Armadas 11, Algeciras. Tel: (95) 666 16 00.

The British Consulate-General, Avda Diagonal 477-13°, 08036 Barcelona. Tel: 322 2151, telex: 52799 a/b 52799 BRBAR E, fax: 322354.

The British Consulate-General, Alameda Urquizo 2-8, 48008 Bilbao. Tel: 415 76 00, telex: 32446 a/b 32446 BRBIL E, fax: 416732.

The British Consulate-General. Plaza Calvo Sotelo 172-1, Apartado 564, Alicante. Tel: (96) 521 60 22.

The British Consulate-General, Avda Isidoro Macabith 45-1, Apartado 307, Ibiza. Tel: (97) 130 18 18.

The British Consulate-General, Edificio Duquesa, Duquesa de Parcent 4-1, Málaga. Tel: (95) 221 75 71.

The British Consulate-General, Plaza Mayor 3D, Palma de Mallorca 12. Tel: (97) 121 24 45.

The British Consulate-General, Paseo de Pereda 27, Santander. Tel: (94) 222 00 00.

The British Consulate-General, Santian 4, Tarragona. Tel: (97) 720 12 46.

The British Consulate-General, Edificio Marichal 5, Suarez Guerra 40, Santa Cruz de Tenerife. Tel: (92) 224 20 00.

The British Consulate-General, Plaza Compostela 23-6, Apartado
    49, Vigo. Tel: (98) 621 14 50.
The British Embassy, calle de Fernando el Santo 16, 28010
    Madrid. Tel: 419 02 00, 419 02 12, telex: 27656 a/b 27656
    INGLA E, fax: 419-0423.
The Spanish Consulate, 21, Rodney St, Liverpool L1 9EF.
The Spanish Consulate, 70 Spring Gardens, Manchester M2 2BQ.
The Spanish Consulate-General, 20 Draycott Place SW3. Tel:
    (071) 581 5921. Residence visas. Tel: (071) 581 5924. Tourist
    visas. Tel: (071) 581 5925. Notary. Tel: (071) 225 0003. Registro
    Civil (day). Tel: (071) 584143. Emergencies (out of hours). Tel:
    (071) 584 5143.
The Spanish Embassy (Chancery), 24 Belgrave Square, London
    SW1X 8QA. Tel: (071) 235 5555.

TRAVEL

Contacts in Britain
British Airways Travel Division, PO Box 115, West London Air
    Terminal, Cromwell Road, London SW7 4ED. Tel: (071) 370
    4255.
British Rail Continental Enquiries. Tel: (071) 834 2345.
Brittany Ferries, Millbay Docks, Plymouth PL1 3EW. Tel: (0752)
    221321. Tel: (0752) 269926 for brochures.
Institute of Spain, 102 Eaton Square SW1. Tel: (071) 235 1485.
Spanish Airlines (IBERIA), Venture House, 29 Glass House St,
    London W1R 5RG.
Spanish Aviation Services, 57B Lupus Street SW1. Tel: (071) 821
    5801.
Spanish National Tourist Office, 57-58 St James St, London SW1.
    Tel: (071) 499 0901.
Trásmediterraneo, Melia Travel, 12 Dover St, London W1. Tel:
    (071) 409 1884.

Contacts in Spain
Ayuda en Carretera (help on the road). Tel: (091) 742 12 13.
Ayuntamientos (Town Halls).
British Airways, Serrano 60-5, 28001 Madrid.
Central de Reservas e Información Internacional, Instituto de la
    Juventud, calle José Ortega y Gasset 71, 28006 Madrid. Tel:
    (091) 401 13 00. (Youth Hostels).
Consejeros de Turismo (Ministers of Tourism, one in each region).

Delegación Española de la Federación Internacional de Camping, Edificio España (grupo 4° 11), 28013 Madrid. Tel: (91) 242 10 89. Camping, discount card and hitchhiking card.

Flebasa Lines, Estación Maritima, Denia (Alicante). Tel: (96) 578 40 11. Connections between Denia and Ibiza, Altea and Formentera.

Iberrail SA, calle Capitán Haya 55, 28020 Madrid. El Andalus.

Información IBERIA. Tel: (91) 411 25 45.

Información RENFE (Spanish Railways), Tel: (91) 411 25 45. Special excursions. Tel: (91) 733 62 00. El Transcantábrico: (91) 253 76 56.

Ministerio de Cultura, Instituto de la Juventud, José Ortega y Gasset 71, 28006 Madrid. Tel: (91) 401 13 00 (Youth or student travel).

Real Automóvil Club de España (RACE), José Abascal 10, 28003 Madrid. The equivalent of the AA.

Secretaria General de Turismo MTTC, calle María de Molina 50, 28006 Madrid. Tels: 411 40 14, 411 60 11, telex: 23284. General information.

TIVE, Fernando el Católico 88, 28015 Madrid. Tel: (91) 232 1300 (Student travel).

ACCOMMODATION

Asociación Nacional de Estaciones Termales (ANET), calle Martin de los Heros 23-4° dcha B, 28008 Madrid. Tel: (91) 542 97 75, fax: 542 98 24. National association of spas.

Cadena Husa, Rambla Cataluna 20, 08007 Barcelona. Tel: (93) 318 13 86, 317 27 00. HUSA Central Booking Office, Paseo de la Castellana 12-6°, 28046 Madrid. Tels: (91) 276 71 86, 275 12 00, telex: 54134. (Chain of hotels).

Familia Hotels, Central de Reservas, calla Canuda 20, 08002 Barcelona (Catalunya). Tel: (93) 317 92 16, telex: 59376, fax: 317 92 16.

Federación Española de Montana, calle Alberto Aguilera 3, 28015 Madrid. Tel: (91) 445 13 82. Mountain refuges.

Hotusa, calle Balmes 12 pral 1, 08007 Barcelona. Tel: (93) 318 45 75, telex: 98201, fax: 318 73 38.

Hotel Puerto de Pajares, Principado de Asturias. PO Box 1348, 33080 Oviedo. Tel: (985) 49 60 23, telex: 84003.

Melia Hotels, calle Princesa 27, 28008 Madrid. Tels: (91) 241 82 00, 241 84 00, fax: 241 19 88. Also 6, Cavendish Square, London

W1M 9HA. Tels: (071) 436 9343, 636 5242, FREEFONE (0800) 282720, fax: 636 72 51.

Novotel, calle Albacete 1, 28037 Madrid. Tel: (91) 405 46 00, telex: 41862 NOVMD, fax: 404 11 05.

Paradores Nacionales, calle Velasquez 18, 28001 Madrid, PO Box 50043, 28082 Madrid. Tels: (91) 435 97 00, 435 97 44, 435 98 14, fax: 435 99 44. Main Reservations. Also, United Kingdom: Keytel International, 402 Edgware Road, London W2 1ED. Tel: (071) 402 8182, telex: 21780. Also, United States: US Marketing Ahead Inc, 433 Fifth Avenue, New York NY10016. Tel: 686 9213, telex: 22 00 26.

Santos Hoteles, calle Juan Bravo 8, Madrid. Tels: (91) 431 21 37, 431 18 97, telex: 41980.

Sol Group, Central de Reservas, Edificio Grupo Sol, calle Gremio Toneleros 42, Poligono San Castello, 07009 Palma de Mallorca. Tels: (871) 29 89 66, 25 20 52, 29 96 540, telex: 68539.

Spanish Property Centre, 2 Alva St, Edinburgh 2. Tel: (031) 226 6633. Also 8 St Bernards Crescent. Tel: (031) 332 8887.

Spanish Property Consultants (Estate Agents), 6 Fernhead Road, London NW4. Tel: (081) 968 7619.

Spanish Property Services, Sunset Lodge, Cedars Close, London NW4. Tel: (081) 203 4140.

Spanish Sun Properties Ltd, 7 The Quadrant, Hoylake, Merseyside. Tel: (071) 628 2484.

TRYP hotels, calle Mauricio Legendre 16, 28046 Madrid. Tel: (91) 315 32 46, telex: 42920 TRYCP E.

CULTURAL, EDUCATIONAL AND SOCIAL

Andalusian Sailing Federation. Tel: (952) 87 03 03.

Andalusian Golf Federation. Tel: (952) 22 59 90.

Andalusian Tennis Federation. Tel: (952) 26 38 39.

Balearic Golf Federation, Avda Rey Jaime III-17 dcha 16, 07012 Palma de Mallorca. Tel: (971) 72 27 53.

Ciudad Universitaria s/n, 28040 Madrid. Tel: (91) 549 77 00. Information about university education.

Central Bureau for Educational Visits and Exchanges, Seymour Mews House, Seymour Mews, London W1H 9PE. Tel: (071) 486 5101.

Consejo Superior de Deportes, Avda Martin Fierro s/n, 28003 Madrid. Tel: (091) 449 73 00, 243 36 06. Sports information.

Federación Española de Actividades Subacuáticos, calle Santaló 15-2°. Barcelona. Underwater sports.
Federación Española de Golf, calle Capitán Haya 9, 28020 Madrid. Tel: (91) 455 26 82, 445 87 15, 455 13 93. Golf.
Federación Española de Vela, calle Juan Vigón 23, Madrid. Tels: (91) 233 53 05, 233 84 08. Sailing.
Govern Balear, Consellería de Turismo, calle Montenegro 5, 07012 Palma de Mallorca. Tel: (971) 71 20 22, telex: 69346 CTIB E.
Ministerio de Culturo (Servicio de Publicaciones), calle Fernando el Católico 77, 28015 Madrid. Tel: (91) 244 56 18. Information.
Ministerio de Educación y Ciencias (MEC), Alcalá 34, 28014 Madrid. Tel: (91) 232 13 00. Ministry of Education.
Servicio de Información del MEC, Alcalá 36, 28014 Madrid. Tels: (91) 521 48 06, 521 45 30, 532 13 00. Information on education.
Relaciones Culturales Internacionales, Ferraz 82 2°, 28008 Madrid. Tel: (91) 479 63 03.
Spanish Club, 5, Cavendish Square, London W1. Tel: (071) 580 2750.
Spanish Embassy Education Office, 20 Peel Street, London W8 7PD. Tel: (071) 727 2462.

BUSINESS CONTACTS

Business contacts in Britain
British Council, 10 Spring Gardens, London SW1. Tel: (071) 930 8466.
Department of Trade and Industry Overseas Trade Division (Spain Desk), 1 Victoria St, London SW1H 0ET. Tels: (071) 215 4284 (Capital goods), 215 5624 (Consumer goods).
Inland Revenue Claims Branch, Foreign Division, Merton Rd, Bootle L69 9BL.
Internal European Policy Division, Department of Trade and Industry, Room 418, 1 Victoria St, London SW1X 0ET. Tel: (071) 215 5354. Certificates of Professional Equivalence.
Spanish Agencies, Mfrs Agent, 160 Castle Hill, Reading. Tel: (0734) 509339.
Spanish Citrus Management Committee, 23 Manchester Square, London W1. Tel: (071) 486 3476.
The Spanish Embassy (Commercial Office), 22 Manchester Square W1. Tel: (071) 486 0101.

Spanish Institute (Instituto de España), 102 Eaton Square, London SW1. Tels: (071) 235 1484, 235 1485.
Spanish Promotion Centre, 23 Manchester Square, London W1. Tel: (071) 935 6140.

Business contacts in Spain

British Chamber of Commerce in Spain, Plaza Santa Barbara 10, 28010 Madrid. Tels: (91) 308 3081/4.
British Council, Plaza Santa Barbara 10, 28010 Madrid. Tel: (091) 319 1250.
British Institute, Almagro 5, 28003 Madrid. Tel: (91) 319 12 50.
Communications General Directorate, calle Ayalá 5, 28001 Madrid. Tel: (91) 448 70 00, fax: 435 55 23.
General Directorate of Customs, calle Guzmán el Bueno 137, 28003 Madrid. Tel: (91) 253 02 00, fax: 233 52 42.
General Directorate of Foreign Commerce, Paseo de la Castellana 162, 28046 Madrid. Tel: (91) 458 00 16, fax: 259 44 66.
General Directorate of Foreign Transactions, Paseo de la Castellana 162, 28046 Madrid. Tel: (91) 259 57 01, fax: 571 16 59.
Income Tax Revenue Bureau, calle Guzmán el Bueno 139, 28020 Madrid. Tel: (91) 250 39 00, fax: 250 51 00.
Industrial Property Registry, calle Panamá 1, 28036 Madrid. Tel: (91) 458 22 00.
Instituto Nacional de la Seguridad Social Subdirección General de Relaciones Internacionales, Padre Damien 4, Madrid 16. The Spanish equivalent of the DSS.
Ministry of Agriculture, Paseo Infanta Isabel 1, 28014 Madrid. Tel: (91) 347 50 00.
Ministry of Economy and Finance, calle Alcalá 9, 28014 Madrid. Tel: (91) 468 20 00, telex: 27811.
Ministry of External Affairs, Plaza de la Provincia 1, 28012 Madrid. Tel: (91) 266 48 00, fax: 266 70 76.
Ministry of Industry and Energy, Paseo de la Castellana 160, 28046 Madrid. Tel: (91) 458 80 10, fax: 457 80 66.
Ministry of Labour and Social Security, calle Augustín de Bethancourt 4, 28003 Madrid. Tel: (91) 253 60 00, fax: 233 29 96.
Spanish Employers' Organisation, calle Diego de León 50, 28006 Madrid. Tel: (91) 563 96 41, fax: 262 80 23.

BRITISH BANKS IN SPAIN

Banco NatWest March SA, Miguel Angel 23, 28010 Madrid. Tel (91) 419 11 12.

Barclays Bank, Madrid Main Branch, Plaza de Colón 1, 28046, Madrid. Tels: (91) 410 2800, 319 9014.

Grindlays Bank, Paseo de la Castilla, 28046 Madrid.

Lloyds Bank International plc, calle Serrano 90, 28006 Madrid. Postal address: Apartado Postal 64, 28080 Madrid.

Midland Bank, 1st Floor Edificio Beatriz, 28006 Madrid. PO Box 2472, calle José Ortega y Gasset 29, Madrid.

LEGAL CONTACTS

Enquiries

The Legal Department, Spanish Embassy, 24 Belgrave Square, London SW1X 8QA. (Background information on buying property in Spain, Spanish succession law and setting up business in Spain).

General: lawyers

Amhurst Brown Colombotti, 2 Duke St, St James's, London SW1Y 6BJ, Tel: (071) 930 2366, telex: 261857, fax (071) 930 2250. Has agents throughout Spain.

Andrews McQueen, 1613 Wimborne Road, Kinson, Bournemouth, Dorset BH11 9AP. Tel: (0202) 582582, fax: (0202) 576262. English solicitors dealing with Spanish law.

T T Bennett, Bennett and Co, Bridge House, 2 Heyes Lane, Alderley Edge, Cheshire SK9 7JY. Tel: (0625) 586937, telex: 585362, fax: 6655566. English solicitors dealing with property and other work in Spain.

Anthony Bertin and Associates, Tontine House, Tontine St, Folkstone, Kent CT20 1UB. Tel: (0303) 46000, telex: 965891 TONLAW. English solicitors with associated offices in Madrid, Málaga and Marbella.

Brooke North and Goodwin, Yorkshire House, East Parade, Leeds LS1 5SD. Tel: (0532) 832100, fax: (0532) 833999. English solicitors and Notaries Public dealing with property and commercial work in Spain and internationally.

Davis Arnold Cooper, 12 Bridewell Place, London EC4 6AD. Tel: (071) 353 6555, fax: (071) 936 2020. Associates: Abogados Ruiz Gallardon de Muniz.

De Beristain Humphrey, Theodore Goddard, 16 St Martins Le Grand, London EC1A 4EJ. Tel: (071) 606 8855, telex: 884678, fax: (071) 606 4390. Associated office in Madrid.

De Pinna Scorers and John Venn, 3 Albemarle St, London W1X 3HF. Tel: (071) 409 3188, telex: 895 1242, fax: (071) 491 2302. English Notaries Public; the firm has contact with Spanish lawyers.

Glaisyers, Alpha Tower, Suffolk St, Queensway, Birmingham B1 1TR. Tel: (021) 632 5881, telex: 338610. Associated offices in various parts of Spain including the Balearics, Barcelona, Marbella, Tenerife, Valencia.

John Howell and Co, 8 Bolton St, Piccadilly, London W1Y 8AU. Tel: (071) 495 2361, fax: (071) 629 4460. Services include conveyancing and other land related work. Associated offices covering most parts of Spain including the Balearic and Canary Islands.

M J Soul, Michael Soul and Associates, 20 Essex St, London WC2R 3AL. Tel: (071) 242 0848, 242 0836, 242 8400, telex: 296342 SOULAW G, fax: 240 2278. Solicitor of the Supreme Court of England and Wales. Associated with offices in Madrid, Barcelona, Marbella, Palma de Mallorca and Málaga.

D W Julian and Co, 14 Kennington Rd, London SE1 7BL. Tel: (071) 928 8021, telex: 261951 JULIAN G, fax: (071) 633 9487. English Notaries Public who have contacts with Spanish lawyers in Madrid, Barcelona, Valencia, Alicante and Málaga.

M E Thomas, Staffurth and Bray, York Road Chambers, Bognor Regis, West Sussex PO21 1LT. Tel: (0243) 864001, fax: 0243 86078. Advises on Spanish property.

Hugh James Jones and Jenkins, Arlbee House, Greyfriars Rd, Cardiff CF1 4BQ. Tel: (0222) 224871, fax: (0222) 388222. Associates in Spain.

Michael Horton and Co, 692 Warwick Rd, Solihull, West Midlands B91 3DX. Tel: (021) 704 2186. English solicitors. Spanish speaking lawyer provides advice on property purchase and notarial services. Costa Brava.

D B Jones, Wallers, Pearl Assurance House, 7 New Bridge St, Newcastle upon Tyne. NE1 8BJ. Deals with exporting advice and setting up businesses in Spain.

Colin Whyman, Champion Miller and Honey, 151 High St, Tenterden, Kent TN30 6JT.

Wilde Sapte, Queensbridge House, 60 Upper Thames St, London EC4V 3BD. Tel: (071) 236 3050, fax: (071) 236 9624.

Some Spanish Lawyers practising in the United Kingdom

L R Barrero, Amhurst Brown Colombotti, 2 Duke St, St James's, London SW1Y 6BJ. Tel: (071) 930 2366, telex: (071) 930 2250, fax: (071) 930 2250. Member of the Madrid Bar, also admitted as Solicitor of the Supreme Court of England and Wales. Preferred fields of practice: property, probate, commercial, general advice on Spanish law.

Canovas Sierra Torres and Co, 11 Yeoman House, The Pavement, Ealing, London W5 4NG. Tel: (081) 566 2567, fax: (081) 566 1903.

Francisco Cantos, Stephenson Harwood, 1 St Paul's Churchyard, London EC1M 8SH. Tel: (071) 329 4422. Member of the Madrid Bar Association.

J B de Abando, 2 Wellington Square, London SW3. Tel: (071) 730 7384, telex: 299778. Member of the Bilbao Bar. Preferred fields of practice: general practice including conveyancing and commercial law.

Antonio de Fortuny, 16 Rex Place, London W1Y 5PP. Tel: (071) 499 2338. Preferred fields of practice: general practice including conveyancing and commercial law.

Jose Maria de Lorenzo, 8/12 New Bridge St, London EC4V 6AL. Tel: (071) 583 6995. Member of the Barcelona Bar. Preferred fields of practice: Personal injuries, property law, probate, matrimonial, commercial law and general advice.

Diaz-Bastien and Truan, 111 Park St, London W1Y 3FB. Tel: (071) 409 2018, fax: (071) 629 2902. Paloma Peman Domecq, Member of the Málaga Bar.

Antonio Irastorza, Boodle Hatfield, 43 Brook St, London W1Y 2BL. Tel: (071) 629 7411, telex: 261414, fax: (071) 629 2621. Member of the Madrid Bar. Also admitted as a solicitor of the Supreme Court of England and Wales.

José Medio and Co, 14 Dover St, London W1X 3PH. Tel: (071) 409 2355, telex: 21551 BROKMI G. Mr Medio: Member of the Oviedo Bar, Mr Prado: Member of the Madrid Bar, Mr Quadra: Member of the Málaga Bar. Preferred fields of practice: general practice including property law, company law, foreign investment in Spain, probate, preparation of Spanish legal documents and taxation law.

Elena Perez Carillo, Bertin Ware and Associates, Tontine House, Tontine St, Folkestone, Kent CT20 1UB. Tel: (0303) 46000.

E Picanol, Bufete Cuatrecasas, 41 Dover St, London W1X 3RB.

Tel: (071) 499 3186, telex: 261576 BERGUL. Member of the
Barcelona Bar. General practice (by appointment only).

Prado, Asua and Co, 9 Young St, Kensington, London W8 5EH.
Tel: (071) 376 0517. Julio Prado LL M, Luis de Asua, Lourdes
Portela, Members of the Madrid Bar Association.

Fernando Scornik, 3rd Floor, 32 St James's St, London SW1A
1HD, Tel: (071) 839 1581, telex: 263593 SELECT-G. Member
of the Las Palmas Bar. Practises in the Canary Islands and visits
London by appointment only.

Jan Malinoski, De Anna Scories and John Venn (Notaries Public),
3 Albermarle St, London W1X 3HF. Tel: (071) 409 3188, fax:
(071) 491 7302. Member of the Barcelona Bar.

Some English lawyers who deal with Spanish law

John Reay-Smith, Al Huerta de Los Naranjos, Peunte Mayorga,
Cádiz.

Agusten Gill de Antunano, Monte Esquinza 26 5 Dcha, 28010
Madrid. Tel: (91) 419 54 31, 419 26 31, telex: 45441. London
office: Stoneham Langton and Passmore, 8 Bolton St,
Piccadilly, London W1Y 8AU. Tel: (071) 499 8000, telex:
21640.

Baker and McKenzie, Pinar 18, Madrid 6. Tel: (91) 411 30 62,
telex: 2280. London office: Aldwych House, Aldwych, London
WC2B 4JP. Tel: (071) 242 6531, telex: 25660, fax: (071) 831
8611.

Brebner and Co, Paseo de la Castellana no 143/2V, 28016 Madrid.
Tel: (91) 270 27 44, 270 27 81. London office: 107 Cheapside,
London EC2V 6DT. Tel: (071) 600 0885, telex: 895 0075
DESK G, fax: (071) 726 2816.

Despatcho Juridico, Castello 128, 28006 Madrid. Tel: (91) 563 10
86, telex: 45060, fax: 563 9976. Mr O C Vero, an English
solicitor admitted to the Spanish Bar. London office: Clifford
Chance, Blackfriars House, 19 New Bridge St, London EC4V
6BY. Tel: (071) 353 0211, telex: 887847.

A V B Grant, Celsa de la Pena Abogados, Almagro 2, 28010
Madrid. Tels: 410 17 64, 410 35 09, 410 02 85, telex: 43278
PLEA E, fax: 410 6586. English solicitor working for a firm of
Spanish lawyers.

Alexander Pitts, Abogados, Goya 63, 28001 Madrid. Tel: 576 52
95, telex: 45581, fax: 575 55 42. English barrister, also admitted
to Spanish Bar.

Frank Porral, Marques del Riscal 11-Dpdo, 28010 Madrid. Tels:

(91) 419 75 75, 419 75 69, telex: 46176 GFCC-E. English barrister, also admitted to Spanish Bar.

R M Smeaton, Gomez-Acebo y Pombo, Castellana 164, Madrid 28046. Tel: 250 72 00, telex: 23429. English solicitor working for a firm of Spanish lawyers.

Stephenson Harwood, Marques del Riscal 11 5, 28010 Madrid. Tel: 410 09 66, telex: 22469, fax: Groups 2 and 3 410 2882. London office: Saddlers' Hall, Gutter Lane, Cheapside, London EC2V 6BS. Tel: (071) 606 7733, telex: 886789 LIMATO G, fax: Groups 2 and 3, (071) 606 0822.

Edward Wiltshire, Lagasca 106, Madrid 6. Tels: 275 03 24, 275 75 27, telex: 46521, fax: 435 40 89. English solicitor.

Peter Herbert Langdon, Linda Vista Baja, calle las Adelfas 216, San Pedro de Alcántara, Málaga.

Ashton Hill Bond, Ricardo Soriena 36 ED, Marias III 2° 208, 29600 Marbella, Málaga. Tel: (91) 177 82 90. Associated offices in Nottingham and London.

V E Callaghan, Apartado 346, Puerto de la Cruz, Tenerife, Canaries. English barrister.

English solicitors in Gibraltar (dealing with Spanish law)
Brooke-North and Goodwin, 2 Irish Place, Gibraltar. Tel: (350) 70545. Leeds Office: Yorkshire House, East Parade, Leeds LS1 5SD. Tel: (0532) 832100.

Glaisyers, 3 Parliament Lane, Gibraltar. Birmingham Office: 10 Rochester Court, Printing House Street, Birmingham B4 6DH.

MISCELLANEOUS

BUPA, 102 Queens Road Brighton BN1 3XT. In Spain: Apartado de Correos 16, 29120 Alhaurin el Grande (Málaga). Tel: (952) 49 11 15.

Danmark AS International Health Insurance, Edificio el Ancla 603, 29640 Fuengirola (Málaga). Tel: (952) 47 12 04, fax: (952) 47 12 08.

Department of Social Security, Overseas Branch, Central Office, Long Benton, Newcastle upon Tyne, NE98 1YX. Tel: (091) 213 50 00.

Employment Services, Overseas Placing Unit (OPS 5), Moorfoot, Sheffield S1 4PQ.

Exeter Hospital Aid Society, 5 Palace Gate Exeter, Devon EX1 1UE.

The Federation of Recruitment and Employment Services Ltd, 36-38 Mortimer St, London WɪN 7RB. SAE appreciated.

Instituto de Proprietarios Extranjeros, Avda de Ifach 1, Edificio el Portál, Calpe (Alicante). Institute of Foreign Property Owners.

Spanish National Radio, 16 Berners St, London Wɪ. Tel: (071) 631 1238.

Spanish and Portuguese Jews Congregation, Lauderdale Road Synagogue, 2 Ashworth Road, London W9. Tel: (071) 289 2573.

Spanish and Portuguese Synagogue, Holland Park, 8 St James Gardens, London Wɪɪ. Tel: (071) 603 3232.

Spanish Catholic Chaplaincy, 47 Palace Court, London W2. Tel: (071) 229 885.

Spanish Commercial and Technical Translations, Marzell House, 116 North End Road, London Wɪ4. Tel: (071) 486 3476.

Spanish Speaking Services, 138 Eversholt St, London NWɪ. Tel: (071) 388 1732)

Spanish Technical Translations Co, 76 Shoe Lane, London EC4. Tels: (071) 583 8690, 353 5813. Translators, interpreters, printers.

Spanish Technical Translation Service, 219 Mortlake Road, Richmond. Tel: (081) 876 7721.

Spanish Technical Translators, 11 Uxbridge Road, London Wɪ2. Tel: (081) 749 3211.

Spanish Television, 16 Berners St, London Wɪ. Tel: (071) 631 3706.

Spanish Translations, 64 Queens St, London EC4. Tel: (071) 248 8707.

CONSUMER AFFAIRS.

Edward McMillan-Scott MEP, Parliamentary Office, Ref EDG004, European Parliament, Rue Belliard, Brussels 1040. Tel: (965) 20 50 00.

FAB—Foreign Advice Bureau, calle Cruz 5, Torremolinos (Málaga). Tels: (952) 383022, 383653, 388736.

Ombudsman (*Defensor del Pueblo*), Señor don Alvaro Gil Robles, calle Eduardo Dato 31, 280210 Madrid. Tels: (91) 319 40 38, 308 28 06.

OMIC (Oficina Municipal de Información al Consumador). Complaints and Information. Local.

Organización de Consumidores y Usarios (OCU), Edocusa, calle Jerez 3-portal C-2°B, 28016 Madrid. Tel: (91) 457 52 07, fax: (91) 457 06 60.

Union de Consumidores de Espana (UCE), Apd 53238, 28080 Madrid. Tel: (91) 435 42 52, 435 46 13. Head office.

PERIODICAL PUBLISHERS

Costa Golf, Apartado 358, Loma de los Riscos 1, Torremolinos (Málaga). Tel: (952) 38 15 42. Monthly.

Green Digest Espana, Glorieta de Pérez Cidón 1-1°B, 28027 Madrid. Tels: (91) 742 74 44, 742 79 53, fax: 32040 16.

Sur in English, Avda Doctor Marañon 48, 28009 Madrid. Tel: (952) 39 39 00, telex: 79013, fax: (952) 27 95 04.

Glossary of Useful Words and Phrases

MONEY

¿Cuánto es?	How much is that?
¿Cuánto vale?	How much is this? (in a shop).
¿Cuánto debe?	How much do I owe you? (in a bar).
¿La dolorosa, por favor?	A very Spanish way of getting the bill and a little old-fashioned which may suggest you have been in the country longer than in actuality.
La cuenta, por favor.	The bill, please (in a restaurant).
¿Para qué es esta cantidad?	What's this amount for?
¿Acepta usted esta tarjeta de crédito?	Do you accept this credit card?
Quédese con el cambio.	Keep the change.
Tráigame la hoja de reclamación.	Bring me a complaint form.

TRAVEL

¿Qué distancia hay hasta . . . ?	How far is it to . . . ?
¿Dónde hay una gasolinera?	Where is there a petrol station?
Llénemelo, por favor.	Fill the tank please.
Siga todo derecho.	Keep straight on.
¿Hay un aparcamiento cerca de aquí?	Is there a car park near here?
¿Puede arreglar este pinchazo?	Can you fix this puncture?
¿Dónde está la playa?	Where's the beach?
correos?	the post office?
la estación?	the station?
el hotel?	the bank?
el teatro?	the theatre?
¿Dónde puedo cambiar dinero?	Where can I change money?
¿Es éste el tren para Madrid?	Is this the train for Madrid?

¿Hace falta cadenas de nieve?
Are snow chains necessary?

Mil pesetas de gasolina, por favor.
1,000 pts worth of petrol please.

¿Tiene agua/aire/aceite?
Have you water/air/oil?

Quiero alquilar un coche para una dia
I want to hire a car for a day.

una semana
a week

Tengo carnet de conducir.
I have a driving licence.

Pidame un taxi, por favor.
Please call me a taxi.
(Give the taxi driver the written address and show him a map.)

¿Hay un autobús al (desde el) aeropuerto?
Is there a bus to (from) the airport?

HOTELS AND ACCOMMODATION

Hemos reservado una habitación doble.
We have booked a double room.

¿Tiene una habitación individual?
Do you have a single room?

¿doble?
double room?

Quiero una habitación con baño.
I want a room with a bath.

con ducha.
with a shower.

con vista.
with a view.

¿Tiene aire acondicionado?
Is there air-conditioning?

¿Puedo ver la habitación?
May I see the room?

¿A que hora se cena?
When is dinner served?

¿Tiene servicio de habitación?
Do you have room service?

GENERAL

giro postal	postal order
hacienda	tax office
declaración	tax return form
entrega personal	personal delivery (by hand)
correo certificado	registered post
Aduana	Customs and Excise
permanencia	permit allowing a stay of a further three months in Spain
residencia	residence permit
certificado de antecedentes penales	certificate of good conduct
matricula	number plate
autovia	by pass
autopista	motorway
letra	form of hire purchase
talón	cheque

caja de ahorros	savings bank
Insalud	Spanish national health service
gasolinera	petrol filling station
comisaria	police station
gestor	official dealing with paperwork
Telefonica	the name of the Spanish telephone service
alcalde	mayor
ayuntamiento	town hall
papel de estado	tax stamp(s)
permisos	permits
permiso de conducción	driving licence
abogado	lawyer
notario	notary
derechos	duties to pay
impuesto	tax
seguro	insurance
contrato	contract
el alquiler	the rent
Quiero alquilar un piso.	I want to rent a flat
¿Conoce uno?	Do you know of one?
Se alquila	for rent
Se vende	for sale
hipoteca	mortgage
escritura (de compraventa)	house conveyance document
Registro de Propriedad	Property Register
Bachillerato	secondary education
Bachiller	school matriculation certificate
formación	training

ABBREVIATIONS

RENFE (Red Nacional de Ferrocarriles Españoles)	State Railway
Cia (Compania)	company
c/ (calle)	street
EE UU (Los Estados Unidos)	USA
GC (Guardia Civil)	Civil Guard
Vd/s (Usted/es)	you (the polite form for an official or a person you do not know well)
IVA	VAT (Value Added Tax)
ITV (Inspección Técnico de Vehiculos)	the Spanish MOT test
SA (Societa Anonima)	a Spanish company

Further Reading

TRAVEL GUIDES

Barrett, Frank and Gill, Chris. *Spain's Hidden Country: A Traveller's Guide* (The Telegraph/Brittany Ferries, 1986). 160pp, illustrated paperback, with maps.

Berlitz Blueprint: Spain (Berlitz, 1989).

Boyd, Alisdair. *The Companion Guide to Madrid and Central Spain* (Collins, 1986). 474pp, illustrated paperback, with maps.

Boyd, Alisdair. *The Essence Of Catalonia: a Traveller's Guide to Barcelona and Its Region* (Deutsch, 1988). 324pp, illustrated paperback, with maps.

Collomb, Robin, G. *Gredos Mountains and Sierra Nevada: Central and Southern Spain* (Walkers Guides, 1987). 96pp, paperback, with maps.

Debelius, Harry. *Spain* (Collins Independent Traveller's Guides, 1988). 320pp, paperback, with maps.

Dell, Catherine. *In Spain* (Nelson, 1985). 80pp, illustrated paperback, with maps.

Ellingham, Mark and Fisher, John. *The Rough Guide to Spain* (Routledge and Kegan Paul, 1985). 400pp, paperback, with maps. Completely revised 2nd edition.

Facaros, Dana. *Spain* (Cadogan Guide, 1987). 480pp, illustrated paperback.

Jacobs, Michael. *A Guide to Andalusia* (Viking, 1990). 400pp, colour illustrations.

Jones, Harold Dennis. *Where to Go in Spain* (Settle, 1988). 156pp illustrated paperback with maps.

Livesey, Herbert B. *Spain* (Mitchell Beazley, 1988) 240pp, illustrated American Express pocket guide, with maps.

Luard, Nicholas. *Andalucia: A Portrait of Southern Spain* (Century, 1984). 288pp, illustrated.

Marvin, Garry. *Coping with Spain* (Basil Blackwell, 1990). 181pp, hardback and paperback with illustrations.

Mandell, Barbara. *Spain: (Off the Beaten Track)* (MPC, 1988). 315pp, illustrated paperback, with maps.

McGirk, Jan. *Exploring Rural Spain* (Christopher Helm, 1988). 167pp, with maps.

Spain (Michelin Tyre Co, 1985). 291pp, illustrated paperback, with maps.

Parker, June. *Walking in Mallorca* (Cicerone, 1986). 144pp, illustrated paperback, with maps.

Spain (A Phaidon Cultural Guide, 1985). 760pp, illustrated, with maps.

Robertson, Ian. *Spain: Blue Guide* (Black, 1989). 598pp, illustrated paperback, with maps. Fifth edition.

Rubesamen, Hans Eckart. *Spain—Costa Brava: Barcelona and the Coastal Resorts* translated from German by David Cocking (RAC Travel Guide, 1990). 96pp, paperback, with colour illustrations and maps.

Steves, Rick. *Spain and Portugal in your Pocket: A Step-by-Step Guide and Travel Itinerary* (Pocket Travellers, Horizon, 1988). 127pp, paperback, with maps.

Thomas, Hugh. *Madrid: A Traveller's Companion* (Constable, 1988). 320pp, illustrated paperback.

Wood, Katie (ed). *Holiday Coastal Spain* (Fontana Holiday Guides, 1989). 371pp, paperback, with maps.

ARTS OF SPAIN

Benarde. *Spanish Ceramic Designs* (Stemmer House (US), 1984). 48pp, paperback, with 82 illustrations.

Franco, J (ed). *Spanish Short Stories: Parallel Text* (Penguin, 1970). Paperback.

Homage to Barcelona: the City and Its Art. 1888-1936 (Arts Council, 1985). 328pp, illustrated paperback.

Jordan, Barry. *Writers and Politics in Franco's Spain (Influence of Politics 1936-1960)* (Routledge 1990). 240pp. Hardback.

Kraus, Dorothy. *The Gothic Choirstalls of Spain* (Routledge and Kegan Paul, 1986). 192pp, illustrated hardback.

Mackay, David. *Modern Architecture in Barcelona. 1854-1939* (BSP Professional, 1989). 119pp, illustrated paperback, with maps.

Newmark (Ed). *Dictionary of Spanish Literature* (Greenwood Press, 1972). 352pp, hardback.

Northup. *Introduction to Spanish Literature* (University of Chicago Press, 1960). 532pp, paperback.

Oliveira, Cezar Claudia. *Madrid Arts Guide* (Art Guide, 1989). 109pp, illustrated paperback, with maps.

Palomino. *Lives of the Eminent Spanish Painters and Sculptors* translated from the Spanish by N A Mallory (Cambridge University Press, 1988). 423pp, illustrated hardback.

Romanillos, Jose L. *Antonio de Torres: Guitar Maker: his Life and Work* (A Nadder Book, 1987). 240pp, illustrated hardback.

Schwartz. *Spanish Film Directors 1950-85: Twenty One Profiles* (Scarecrow Press, 1986). 253pp, paperback with 133 illustrations.

Takacs, *Spanish Genre Painting in the Seventeenth Century* translated from Hungarian Akad Kiado (Budapest, 1983). 283pp, illustrated hardback.

Ward, Philip. *Oxford Companion to Spanish Literature* (Oxford University Press, 1978). 638pp, hardback.

PALACES

Brown, Jonathan. *A Palace for a King: The Buen Retiro and the Court of Philip IV (Madrid)* (Yale, 1986). 320pp, illustrated paperback.

Rosenthal, Earl E. *The Palace of Charles V in Granada* (Princeton University Press, 1985). 320pp, illustrated hardback, with 61 plates.

Trevelyan, Raleigh. *Shades of the Alhambra (Granada)* (The Folio Society, 1984). 127pp, illustrated. (Secker and Warburg, 1985), 128pp, illustrated.

GEOGRAPHY OF SPAIN

Busselle, Michael. *Landscape in Spain* (Pavilion, 1988). 159pp, illustrated, photographs by Michael Busselle, commentary by Nicholas Luard.

Casa Valdes, Marquesa de. *Spanish Gardens* translated from the Spanish by Edward Tanner (Antique Collectors' Club, 1987). 299pp, illustrated, with maps.

Rose, David. *Beneath the Mountains: Exploring the Deep Caves of Asturias* (Hodder & Stoughton, 1987). 192pp, illustrated, with maps, 8 colour plates.

LIVING IN SPAIN

Ballard, Sam and Jane. *Paradores of Spain: Unique Lodgings in State-owned Castles, Convents, Mansions and Hotels* (Moorland, 1986). 241pp, illustrated paperback, with maps.

Blackstone Franks Guide to Living in Spain (Kogan Page, 1988). 208pp, with map.

Brown, Karen. *Spanish Country Inns and Paradors* (Harrap Columbus, 1987). 272pp, illustrated paperback.

Busselle, Michael. *Castles in Spain: A Traveller's Guide featuring the National Parador Inns* (Pavilion, 1989). 239pp, illustrated with maps.

Kite, Cynthia. *Spanish Country Inns and Paradors* (Columbus, 1987). 256pp, illustrated paperback, with maps.

Reay-Smith, John. *Living in Spain* (Hale, 1986). 207pp, illustrated, with maps, and 16 plates.

Spanish Property: A Buyer's Bible (McMillan, Bennett, 1988). 40pp, paperback, with map.

Svensson, Per. *Your Home in Spain: Before and After Purchase* (Institute of Foreign Property Owners, 1987). 200pp, illustrated paperback, with one map. 3rd edition.

Tinsley, Teresa. *Time Off in Spain and Portugal* (Horizon, 1989).

Williams, N Scarlyn. *Teach Yourself Spanish* (Edinburgh University Press, 1966).

NATURAL HISTORY

Busby, John. *Birds in Mallorca* (Christopher Helm, 1988). 128pp.

Grunfeld, Frederic V. *Wild Spain: A Travellers and Naturalists Handbook* (Ebury, 1988). 222pp, illustrated paperback, with maps.

Innes, Clive. *Wild Flowers of Spain* (Cockatrice, 1987). 64pp, illustrated paperback.

Polunin, Oleg. *Flowers of South-West Europe: A Field Guide* (Oxford University Press, 1988). 480pp, illustrated paperback, with maps.

Tomkies, Mike. *In Spain's Secret Wilderness* (Cape, 1989). 224pp, 32 plates, and colour photographs.

SPANISH FOOD AND DRINK

Aris. *Recipes from a Spanish Village* (Conran Octopus, 1990). 144pp, illustrated.

Azner and Froud. *Home Book of Spanish Cooking* (Faber, 1974). 224pp, paperback.

Butcher. *Spanish Kitchen* (Macmillan, 1990). 320pp, illustrated.

Evans, Sarah Jane. *Travellers Guide to the Spanish Menu* (Absolute Press, 1985). Paperback.

Fahy. *Little Spanish Cook Book* (Appletree Press, 1990). 60pp, with 30 colour illustrations.

Jessell. *Taste of Spain: Traditional Spanish Recipes and their Origins* (IB Tauris, 1990). 160pp, colour illustrations.

Read, Jan. *Pocket Guide to Spanish Wine* (Mitchell Beazley, 1988). 160pp, illustrated.

Snell. *202 Spanish Wines* (Lookout Publications, Spain 1987). 124pp, illustrated paperback.

Stewart, Carole. *Self-catering in Spain: Making the Most of the Local Food and Drink* (Croom Helm, 1986). 144pp, illustrated paperback.

PERSONAL ACCOUNTS OF LIFE IN SPAIN

A Day in the Life of Spain. Photographed by 100 of the world's leading photo journalists on one day, May 7th 1987 (Collins, 1988). 220pp, chiefly illustrations, with maps.

Borrow, George. *The Bible in Spain: Or, the Journeys, Adventures, and Imprisonments of an Englishman in an Attempt to Circulate the Scriptures in the Peninsula* (originally published John Murray, 1843) (Century Travellers Series, 1985). 510pp, paperback. This is a fascinating account of journeys in Spain some 150 years ago. The writing is beautifully descriptive and religion is kept to a minimum. Many of the comments on politicians, regional characteristics, personalities in the public eye, and general conditions are as true today as then and help to explain the lack of education and knowledge that still exists. It is written from the point of view of a much travelled Englishman. One admires his courage.

Braithwaite, Belinda. *A Girl, a Horse and a Dog* (Collins, 1988). 236pp, illustrated, with 12 plates and 1 map.

Brenan, Gerald. *South from Granada* (originally published Hamish Hamilton, 1957) (Folio Society, 1988). 278pp, 14 leaves of plates.

Chetwode, Penelope. *Two Middle-Aged Ladies in Andalusia* (originally published John Murray, 1963) (Century Travellers Series, 1985). 288pp, illustrated paperback.

Davies, Hugh Seymour. *The Bottlebrush Tree: A Village in Andalusia* (Constable, 1988). 208pp.

Gala, Antonio. *El Manuscrito Carmesi* (Planeta, Spain 1990). A Spanish best-seller treating of the Conquest of Granada from the point of view of the last Arab ruler.

Hooper, John. *The Spaniards: a Portrait of the New Spain* (Viking, 1986). 288pp, illustrated, with maps.

Lee, Laurie. *As I Walked Out One Midsummer Morning 1935-36* (Deutsch, 1969). 191pp, illustrated, with map.

Lewis, Norman. *Voices of the Old Sea (1945-50) (Catalonia)* (Hamish Hamilton, 1984). 202pp.

Luard, Nicholas. *Andalucia: A Portrait of Southern Spain (1972-1980)* (Century, 1985). 288pp, illustrated paperback.

Luke, Peter. *The Mad Pomegranate & The Praying Mantis: an Andalusian Adventure (1967-1977)* (Mantis, 1984). 238pp.

Macaulay, Rose. *Fabled Shore: From the Pyrenees to Portugal* (originally published Hamish Hamilton, 1949) (Oxford University Press, 1986). 248pp, illustrated paperback, with 8 plates.

Morris, Ian. *Spain* (originally published Faber, 1979) (Barrie and Jenkins, 1988). 207pp, colour illustrations and 1 map.

O'Brien, Kate. *Farewell Spain (1936-37)* (originally published Heinemann, 1937) (Virago, 1985). 229pp, illustrated with drawings.

Pritchett, V.S. *The Spanish Temper* (Hogarth Press, 1984). 224pp, paperback.

Walker, Ted. *In Spain* (Secker & Warburg, 1987). 280pp, 1 map.

Winsland, Elaine. *Ibiza Was My Home* (Book Guild, 1989). 180pp, illustrated.

SOCIAL AND POLITICAL HISTORY

Blinkhorn, Martin. *Spain in Conflict 1931-1939: Democracy and Its Enemies* (Sage, 1986). 304pp, illustrated.

Borkenau, Franz. *The Spanish Cockpit: An Eyewitness Account of the Political and Social Conflicts of the Spanish Civil War* (Liberation Classics) (originally published Faber, 1937) (Pluto, 1986). 320pp, paperback.

Carr, Raymond. *The Civil War in Spain (1936-39)* (Weidenfeld & Nicolson, 1986). 328pp, paperback, with maps.

Clark, Bob. *No Boots to my Feet: Experiences of a Britisher in Spain 1937-38* (Student Bookshops Ltd, 1984). 120pp, illustrated paperback.

Collins, Roger. *The Arab Conquest of Spain: 710-797 (A History of Spain)* (Basil Blackwell, 1989). 239pp.

Cunningham, Valentine (ed). *Spanish Front: Writers on the Civil War* (Oxford University Press, 1986). 320pp, illustrated paperback.

Dillard, Heath. *Daughters of the Reconquest: Women in Castilian Town Society 1100-1300* (Cambridge University Press, 1984). 272pp, illustrated.

Edmonds Lloyd. *Letters from Spain* ed Amirah Inglis (Allen and Unwin, 1985). 216pp, illustrated with 1 map.

Fletcher, R A. *The Quest for El Cid* (Hutchinson, 1989). 220pp, illustrated, with maps.

Foweraker, Joe. *Making Democracy in Spain: Grass Roots Struggle in the South 1955-1975* (Cambridge University Press, 1989). 289pp, with 1 map.

Fusi-Aizpurua, Juan Pablo. *Franco: A Biography* translated by Felipe Fernandez-Armesto (Unwin Hyman, 1987). 202pp, illustrated, with maps.

Gilmour, David. *The Transformation of Spain: From Franco's Dictatorship to the Constitutional Monarchy (1939-1984) (Quartet, 1985). 320pp.*

Gregory, Walter. *The Shallow Grave: A Memoir of the Spanish Civil War* (Gollancz, 1986). 192pp, illustrated, with maps.

Gunther, Richard. *Spain after Franco: The Making of a Competitive Party System* (University of California Press, 1988). 509pp, illustrated paperback, with map.

Haigh, R H, Morris, D S, and Peters, A R (eds). *The Guardian Book of the Spanish Civil War* (Wildwood House, 1987). 332pp, with maps.

Irving, Washington. *Chronicles of the Conquest of Granada* (Oxford University Press, 1829).

Krasikov, Anatalii. *From Dictatorship to Democracy: Spanish Reportage* translated by N Shartse (Pergamon, 1984). 227pp, illustrated.

Lalaguna, Juan. *A Travellers History of Spain* line drawings by John Hoste (Windrush, 1990). Illustrated paperback.

Lancaster, Thomas D, and Prevost, Gary (eds). *Politics and Change in Spain* (Praeger, 1985). 224pp, illustrated, with 1 map.

Lovett, A W. *Early Habsburg Spain 1517-1598* (Oxford University Press, 1986). 300pp, paperback, with maps.

Martin, Colin, and Parker, Geoffrey. *The Spanish Armada* (Penguin, 1989). 269pp, illustrated paperback.

Martin Paula. *Spanish Armada Prisoners: The Story of the Nuestra Senora del Rosario and her Crew, and of other prisoners in England 1587-97* (Exeter University Publications, 1988). 113pp, illustrated.

Matthews, John. *El Cid: Champion of Spain* plates by James Field (Firebird, 1988). 48pp, illustrated with 1 map.

Mattingley Garrett, *The Defeat of the Spanish Armada* (Cape, 1983). 384pp, illustrated. 2nd edition.

McDonogh, Gary Wray. *Good Families of Barcelona: A Social History of Power in the Industrial Era* (Princeton University Press, 1986). 262pp, illustrated, with maps.

McKee, Alexander. *From Merciless Invaders: The Defeat of the Spanish Armada* (Souvenir, 1987). 288pp, illustrated, with maps.

Milne-Tyte, Robert. *Armada! The Planning, the Battle and After* (Hale, 1988). 160pp, paperback, with maps.

Noel, Gerard. *Ena, Spain's English Queen* (Constable, 1984). 323pp, illustrated.

Orwell, George. *Homage to Catalonia: And, Looking Back on the Spanish War* (Penguin in Association with Secker and Warburg, 1966, 1984 printing). 246pp, paperback.

Parker, Geoffrey. *Philip II* (originally published Hutchinson, 1979) (Cardinal, 1988). 238pp, paperback with 1 map.

Pollack, Benny. *The Paradox of Spanish Foreign Policy: Spain's International Relations from Franco to Democracy* (Pinter, 1987). 200pp.

Preston, Paul (ed). *Revolution and War in Spain 1931-1939* (Methuen, 1986). 299pp, paperback.

Preston, Paul. *The Triumph of Democracy in Spain* (Methuen, 1986). 288pp, paperback.

Pridman, Geoffrey. *The New Mediterranean Democracies: Regime Transition in Spain, Greece and Portugal (1975-1983)* (Cass, 1984). 193pp, illustrated, with maps.

Rubottom, R Richard. *Spain and the United States: Since World War II* (Praeger, 1984). 163pp.

Share, Donald. *The Making of Spanish Democracy* (Praeger, 1986). 230pp.

Smyth, Denis. *Diplomacy and Strategy of Survival: British Policy and Franco's Spain 1940-41)* (Cambridge University Press, 1988). 560pp.

Stradling, R A. *Philip IV and the Government of Spain 1621-1665*

(Cambridge University Press, 1988). 615pp, illustrated, with 1 map.

SPANISH ECONOMICS AND LAW

Credades, Bernado M (ed). *Spanish Business Law* (Kluwer Law & Taxation, 1985). 656 pp.

Donaghy, P J, and Newton, Michael T. *Spain: A Guide to Political and Economic Institutions* (Cambridge University Press, 1987). 242pp, illustrated paperback.

Harris, Robert Joseph. *The Spanish Economy in the 20th Century* (Croom Helm series on the contemporary economic history of Europe, 1985). 207pp.

Ringrose, David R. *Madrid and the Spanish Economy 1560-1850* (University of California Press, 1983). 405pp, illustrated, with maps.

Sanchez-Albornoz, Nicolas. *The Economic Modernization of Spain 1830-1930* translated by Karen Powers and Manuel Sanudo (New York University Press, 1987). 295pp, illustrated, with 1 map.

Tamames, Ramon. *The Spanish Economy: An Introduction* (Hurst, 1986). 274pp, illustrated, with maps.

RELIGION

Christian, William A. *Local Religion in Sixteenth Century Spain* (Princeton University Press, 1989). 283pp, illustrated paperback, with map.

Lannon, Frances. *Privilege, Persecution and Prophecy: The Catholic Church in Spain 1875-1975* (Clarendon, 1987). 350pp, with 2 maps.

Payne, Stanley G. *Spanish Catholicism: An Historical Overview* (University of Wisconsin Press, 1984). 263pp.

BULLFIGHTING

Collins, Larry and Lapierre, Dominique. *Or I'll Dress you In Mourning (El Cordobes)* (Weidenfeld and Nicolson, 1968, 1988 printing). 349pp, illustrated paperback, with 24 plates.

Marvin, Garry. *Bullfight* (Basil Blackwell, 1988). 244pp, illustrated.

Index